How To Build
Fences
& Gates

By the Editors of Sunset Books
and Sunset Magazine

LANE BOOKS · MENLO PARK, CALIFORNIA

Design Credits

Armstrong and Sharfman, Landscape Architects: pp. 12 (top), 70 (top), 94 (bottom left). Robert Babcock, Landscape Architect: p. 72 (top left). Baldwin, Eriksson, and Peters, Landscape Architects: p. 58 (center left). Baronian and Danielson, landscape architects: p. 61 (top). Douglas Baylis, Landscape Architect: pp. 33 (bottom right), 51 (top right). Harold Bessner, Jr.: p. 65. John S. Bolles: p. 49 (center left). Elizabeth Brazeau, Landscape Architect: p. 61 (bottom left). Jack Buktanica, Landscape Architect: pp. 62, 71 (bottom left). A. O. Bumgardner and Partners, Architects: p. 89 (top right). California Redwood Association: pp. 16-17, 23 (bottom). Warren Callister, Architect: p. 85 (bottom right). Campbell and Wong, Architects: p. 81 (bottom right). John A. Carter: p. 73 (center left). Chaffee-Zumwalt and Associates, Landscape Architects: p. 41 (center left). Robert Chittock, Landscape Architect: p. 74. Thomas Church, Landscape Architect: pp. 49 (top right), 50 (bottom left), 68. Robert Cornwall, Landscape Architect: p. 70 (bottom left). J. E. Costello: p. 9 (center). W. Bennett Covert: p. 71 (top right). John M. Davis, Architect: pp. 42 (top), 70 (bottom right). Jocelyn Domela and Associates, Landscape Architects: p. 69 (left, right). Eckbo, Royston, and Williams, Landscape Architects: pp. 40 (center right), 51 (bottom left). Chandler Fairbank: p. 13 (top). John N. Field: p. 87 (right). Philip Fisk, Architect: p. 40 (center left). George Fuller, Landscape Designer: p. 70 (center left, center right). C. Jacques Hahn, Landscape Architect: p. 38 (left). Walter A. Hansen, Architect: pp. 84, 88 (top). G. H. Hayes: p. 72 (bottom left). Keith Hellstrom, Landscape Architect: p. 50 (center right). Albert W. Hilgers: p. 41 (bottom right). Glen Hunt and Associates, Architects: pp. 39, 61 (center right). Chuck Ito, Landscape Architect: pp. 55 (left), 56 (top left). R. W. Jones, Landscape Architect: p. 48 (top right). Jones and Peterson, Landscape Architects: pp. 82 (bottom right), 83 (top right), 85 (center left). William Louis Kapranos, Landscape Architect: pp. 71 (center left), 72 (top right), 92 (right). Casey A. Kawamoto, Landscape Architect: p. 56 (top right). E. Leslie Kiler, Landscape Architect: p. 91 (top right). George Knight, Knight Lumber Company: p. 40 (bottom left). Roy Krell: p. 51 (center left). Robert Krutcher: p. 73 (center right). Ernest J. Kump and Associates, Architects: p. 89 (bottom right). Frederick M. Lang: p. 41 (top right). W. Leighton: p. 41 (bottom left). Linesch and Reynolds, Landscape Architects: p. 61 (bottom right). Ian Mackinley and Associates, Architects: p. 92 (left). Leonard H. McGuire: p. 51 (center right). Donald D. McMurray, Architect: p. 32 (bottom left). George Murata, Landscape Architect: p. 60. Bob Nelson, Northern California Fence Company: p. 75 (right). Edward Nelson: p. 12 (bottom). Vladimir Ossipoff and Associates, Architects: p. 79 (left). Richard W. Painter, Landscape Designer: p. 51 (top left). Alfred Preis, Architect: p. 58 (center right). Robert Billsborough Price, Architect: pp. 51 (bottom right), 61 (center left). Ribera and Sue, Landscape Architects: p. 43 (right). Gil Rogers: pp. 45 (bottom), 88 (bottom left). Dan L. Rowland, Architect: pp. 59 (top left), 72 (bottom right). Royston, Hanamoto, Beck, & Abey, Landscape Architects: p. 48 (top left). Roy Rydell, Landscape Architect: p. 45 (top). Toshio Saburomaru: p. 94 (top). Burton Schutt: p. 94 (center right). Geraldine Knight Scott, Landscape Architect: p. 87 (left). Michael Siegel: p. 91 (bottom left). Sewall Smith: p. 9 (bottom). Splenda and Yamamoto, Landscape Architects: pp. 41 (top left), 50 (top), 71 (top left). Allan Steinau, Architect: pp. 14, 46 (right). John W. Storrs, Architect: p. 82 (top right). Charles Sumner, Architect: p. 91 (top right). Roland Terry, Architect: p. 49 (bottom right). Henry Van Siegman, Landscape Architect: pp. 38 (right), 44 (center). Willis and Associates, Inc., Architects: p. 60. Yocho Council, Landscape Architects: p. 82 (top left).

Edited by Donald W. Vandervort

Special Consultant: Lee Klein

Design: Lawrence A. Laukhuf.

Artwork: Most of the artwork in this book is by Joe Seney.
E. D. Bills did the illustrations on pages 16, 17, 20 (right),
21 (left), 22, 23, 28, 73, 90.

Cover: Fence and gate designed by Paul Hayden Kirk of
Kirk, Wallace, McKinley AIA & Associates, Seattle, Washington.
Photograph by Don Normark.

Ninth Printing February 1975
Executive Editor, Sunset Books: David E. Clark

Contents

POST AND RAIL fence clearly defines entrance road.

Fences and Their Functions

Most people rarely notice fences until they decide to build one. Then, as they begin looking with more than just a casual interest, the diversity in fencing becomes readily apparent. There are almost as many different fences as there are people who build them. Fences range from pickets to boards to wire, and each type of fence fulfills a very specific function.

On the surface, particular types of fences may look alike. On closer examination, however, there are individual characteristics which distinguish one from another. The neat and traditional white picket fence varies from the plain prow-shaped Gothic style to a seemingly endless variety of top patterns. Board fences may have vertical or horizontal boards. They can be tailored with a tongue-and-groove construction, ruggedly constructed of rustic boards butted together, or built with open or battened spaces between the boards.

Fences are built for many reasons; therefore it is advantageous to begin with a discussion of the purposes of fences.

FIRST THINGS FIRST

Traditionally the two most important reasons for building a fence have been to define a boundary line and to provide security. But the increase in outdoor living has been responsible for several new concepts concerning the role fencing is to play. For example, fences can be used to control wind and sun problems, to create sheltered pockets to catch the sun, or to act as screens to keep out prevailing winds. Just as walls are used indoors to divide up the house, fences and screens can be used outdoors to separate areas of work, play, and storage. Visually, a fence can be as essential an element in a landscape plan as can a tree or a vine.

The closeness of modern living has also increased the need for privacy; fences and screens are often the quickest and easiest means of achieving this.

When a fence functions as a wall of an outdoor room, it can be decorated like an interior wall. Decorative panels, designs, and complementary plantings are some of the devices you can consider.

Before choosing a fence you must first determine the role it is to perform.

Security

Fencing in pioneer days gave protection from Indian attacks and from wild animals. However,

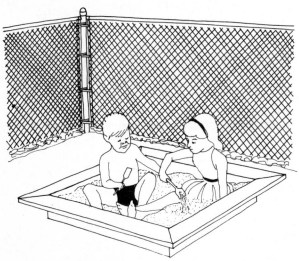

SAFETY OF CHILDREN has always been among the major reasons for planning and building a fence.

as settlers spread throughout the land and those dangers diminished, fences gradually became more decorative than protective.

In recent years, the role of security has assumed renewed importance in both residential and commercial fencing. At the same time, new developments in security fencing (such as the metal chain link) have given security-conscious fence builders more alternatives from which to choose.

Privacy

Today, privacy is of primary importance to many homeowners in their selection of fences and screens. The degree of privacy desired will influence your choice of materials. For example, solid

panels, close-set grapestakes, boards, and basket weave can give you maximum screening and privacy. Partial privacy can be achieved through the use of some plastics, vertical louvers, slat, and wire with plantings. Fencing materials that offer little or no privacy are clear plastics, glass, lattice, bare wire, and post and rail.

Of course the easiest way to achieve total privacy is to rim the property with a high, solid fence. Once the fence is up, however, the homeowner may discover that he has created a rigid environment with a confined, boarded-up feeling.

Through imaginative placing of fences, screens, and plants, it is possible to create your own private world. The Japanese are masters at this and many of the most attractive gardens in the West have been strongly influenced by them.

Another way of sidestepping the use of a solid, high boundary fence is the employment of selective screening. A combination of high and low, open and closed fences and screens usually does the job quite nicely. Solid panels can be built into the fence where the line of sight needs to be interrupted. Where a view is desired, sections of the fence can be left partially open, using rails, lattice, wire, plastic, or glass.

In areas where a solid fence or screen is essential, consideration of what your neighbor has to look at is important. There are several varieties of fences that look nice on both sides (see page 49).

DESIRE FOR PRIVACY has been an important factor in the development of tall fence screening.

Planting on both sides can also help to transform an unfriendly wall into an attractive addition to the landscape.

Environmental Control

Another important consideration in planning fence and screen installations is environmental control. Three of the most common environmental factors to contend with are wind, sun, and noise. Through the use of fences and screens, the intensity of these elements can be modified to create an enjoyable, livable outdoor space.

Protection against the sun. Heat and glare from the sun can be controlled in several ways. Glare can be reduced through the use of plastic panels or glare-reducing glass. These materials can also turn dark corners into softly lighted areas. For dappled shade, sunlight can be filtered through a louvered, slat, or basket weave fence or trellis. A vertical sun screen around a patio will keep out the late afternoon sun that slants in under trees and roof overhangs. This type of screen can also be used to cool the western wall of a house by stopping or filtering the sun before it reaches the walls and windows.

Screening against wind. The wind is not as easy to control as the sun because its behavior is less predictable. Before you build a screen or fence for wind control purposes you should understand the wind's behavior in your yard. The prevailing direction of the wind in a certain area is not necessarily the direction it will blow through your garden. Houses—and other large objects such as fences—can act as giant baffles and the action of the wind in a garden can be affected by the fence's relationship to the house. Before planning a wind screen, it's a good idea to chart garden wind currents by hanging small flags about the yard and noting their movements during windy periods.

There are normally two choices in selecting materials for wind control structures. Glass might seem a logical choice for preserving a view as well as controlling the wind but, surprisingly, it is seldom the most efficient material for wind control. A wind screen made of closely-woven slats or one with a slanting baffle on top will break up a strong wind more efficiently. (See wind tests information on page 8.)

Reducing noise. A problem which has been receiving more and more attention in recent years—especially in urban areas—is noise. Homeowners near freeways and highly traveled streets often wonder if there is something they can do with fences or screens to reduce traffic sounds.

Unfortunately, acoustics experts don't impart much hope to homeowners. Certain structures are effective in reducing noise levels, but only minimally. To be effective, a barrier must be solid and heavy (thickness and mass are important). It should also extend several feet above the source of the sound and the receiver—the higher the better.

Many people agree that there is some psychological satisfaction to be derived from visually removing the source of sound from the receiver. Thus, the placement of screens, hedges, plants, and trees along property fronting a highway might make it *seem* quieter even though measurements of noise levels would show no (or maybe just a negligible) reduction.

WIND CONTROL can be achieved with the installation of a screen made of closely-woven slats.

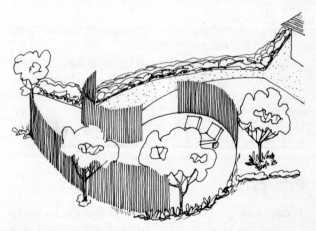

OUTDOOR ROOMS can be created in garden areas with the help of fences and screens in varied styles.

Creating an Outdoor Room

As living space becomes more valuable, many homeowners look for ways of reclaiming and re-organizing unused areas of their gardens. Through the use of fences and screens, this space can be made into attractive outdoor rooms.

Short, free-standing fences and screens can effectively separate the outdoor living area from the service area, gardening center, and play yard, thereby providing usable and separate areas for work, play, and relaxation. See-through materials such as lath or wire make good play yard boundaries. Lath or spaced slat is an excellent choice for screening off garden work centers and swimming pool equipment. One homeowner's solution for hiding an unattractive pile of machinery near his swimming pool was to screen it from view with a narrowly spaced, tall slat screen, backlighted at night to create an interesting visual feature.

In the creation of an outdoor room, the trees, sky, neighboring houses, and landscape beyond, are elements that must be considered. Some may be screened out or incorporated into the plan. Placement of a narrow screen in a specific place may be all that's needed to blot out an objectionable power pole. If the land slopes down to a busy street or freeway, a low horizontal screen can conceal the road below yet provide an unobstructed view of the hills beyond. A neighbor's bird's-eye view of your yard (and *your* view of *him*) can be blocked by an overhead horizontal screen.

There are no hard and fast rules to follow in the selection and use of fencing and screening to create outdoor rooms. A small lot surrounded by a large boundary fence may seem larger and less confining if a panel or divider made of another material is added between the house and the fence. On the other hand, a large yard may become more intimate and inviting if it's broken up with interior screening.

Whatever the type or style of screening you choose, it should relate to the garden as a unit and not stand alone as an apparent afterthought. Choose only those materials that will harmonize with the feeling, tone, and scale of the garden and house and the entire landscape design.

Give Your House a "Face-Lifting"

Through imaginative and attractive placement of screens and plantings, the outward appearance of a home can be completely transformed. Often this approach can be used to give new life to a dated facade or to impart some individuality to a tract home. This new face is often the by-product of creating an outdoor room in the front yard.

Screens used to hide objectionable features need not be solid, formidable structures designed to completely block the house from view. Instead, they can have open spaces and can be combined with selective plants to mellow and enhance the appearance of the house.

Local ordinances in some communities set definite limitations on the height of screens and fences that can be used between the front of the house and the street. Be sure to check local building regulations before starting a project of this kind.

FREE-STANDING SCREENS separate outdoor spaces into usable and distinct areas for work or for play.

OUTWARD APPEARANCE of house can be transformed with careful placement of screens, plantings.

WIND TESTS—WHICH FENCES PERFORM BEST?

Erecting a solid barrier might seem to be the best answer to wind problems, but experts conducting a long series of wind tests have proven that this is not necessarily true. As the sketch below shows, a solid fence tends to create an eddy which has a tendency to pull the main flow of wind down to ground level.

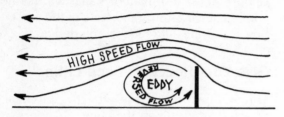

FIG. 1

In most situations, it is not necessary to completely stop the wind. What is important is a rise in the comfort temperature—a complex measurement of the factors that affect your comfort (temperature of the air, velocity of the wind, relative humidity, etc.). Through these factors, comfort temperature becomes the temperature you feel. For example, you will feel chillier in a high wind even though the thermometer may remain at a constant 65°.

The tests illustrated were made outdoors with full-sized fence panels and in a wind tunnel with scale models. Readings of the comfort temperature were first taken in the direct path of the wind, and then with the test fences across the wind. Comparative readings showed how much difference the fence made. The more efficient the fence performed as a wind screen, the more it raised the comfort temperature.

The results of the tests did not give clear cut answers to every wind problem, because the adequacy of a fence can only be measured as to how it fulfills its specific function. Sunbathing or dining comfortably might call for a different type of wind control than for playing tennis. There are also situations in which you want to encourage the flow of air rather than inhibit it.

If you know how you want a fence to perform for a particular wind problem, the accompanying sketches may be helpful. Marks at each 2-foot

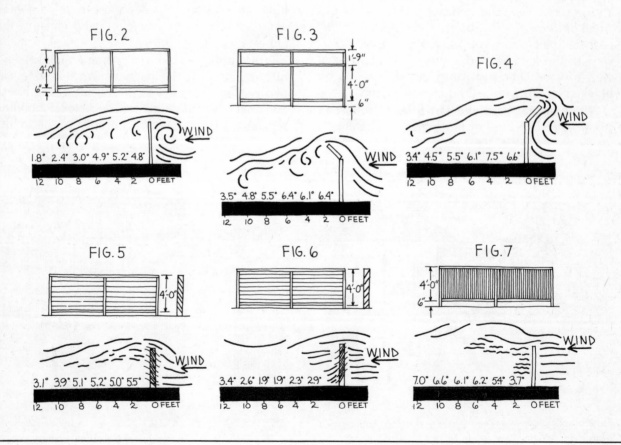

interval indicate how much higher—in degrees—the comfort temperature was at that spot with the fence in place than it was without it. Here are the results:

The reverse flow, or eddy, which forms with a solid fence (figure 1) makes it a poor choice where wind is a problem. When a space is left at the bottom of the solid fence (figure 2) the performance is better because the flow of air at ground level inhibits formation of the eddy. Maximum protection for this fence comes at a distance about equal to the height of the fence. When a baffle, angled at 45°, is added (figure 3), the area of protection is increased considerably. Maximum protection is at a distance equal to slightly more than the height of the fence. Tests were also made with the baffle placed at other angles and slanted toward the wind (figure 4)—this is the type of wind barrier used aboard ship to protect the bridge. This barrier gave greatest wind protection to the area near the fence. The louver fence tested (figure 5) gave the best protection over the greatest distance, though the increase in comfort temperature was not as great as with other fence types. With the louvers reversed (figure 6) the protection was predictably less because the wind was directed right into the area to be protected. The vertical lath fence (figure 7) gave the most unexpected results—the lowest reading was close to the fence and highest was 12 feet away. The reasons for this is that the laths diffuse the wind. That which goes through comes out at jet-like speeds and dissipates in the first foot or so. From there it forms a slow-moving cushion of air which acts as a ceiling and prevents the air moving over the top of the fence from coming down into the protected area.

Conclusions. As you can see, the tests didn't prove conclusively that any one fence gave decidedly better protection than all others for an overall set of problems. But they did point out the following facts:

1. The solid fence is usually not the best for wind control.

2. A screen-like fence, such as the slat fence, will protect a wider area than its openness would suggest possible.

3. Movable louvers offer interesting possibilities—the protection received is, of course, dependent upon the position of the louvers. Louvers directed down might be used to catch cool summertime breezes.

OPEN FENCES with slats placed horizontally and vertically are effectively used for wind control.

GLASS PANELS provide protection from wind, do not interfere with panoramic ocean view beyond.

SLAT OVERHEAD deflects the wind and creates a warm and sheltered area for swimmers and loungers.

Fence Plantings

Fences and plants normally go hand in hand. A fence is a natural backdrop for plant material, which in turn can soften the rigid lines of boundary fences. Plants alone can often function adequately and effectively as a fence or screen but, because of the time it takes for plants to grow, many homeowners would rather build a permanent fence which will accomplish the screening job immediately. This conflict can be solved by using temporary fencing that can be removed when the plants mature. At that time, fence posts can be left in place (shortened to about three feet) and used to support wires or mesh screening.

Many permanent fences can be effectively used to complement and display plantings. A plain board fence may gain in attractiveness when placed so that portions of it will disappear behind lush foliage, thereby breaking up its rigid, horizontal top line. Shrubs or vines espaliered against a simple fence can create a different texture.

Fences can also be used as climate modifiers for plants, i.e., to break the prevailing wind, or to cast shade in a garden that might have too much sun for certain kinds of plants.

For frost protection a fence should be designed with openings to let cold air out. Frigid air acts like water—it flows downhill and piles up behind obstacles. A solid fence at a low point in the garden may dam up cold air, damaging plants. Either a space should be left between the bottom of the fence and the ground, or a gate should be put in that can be opened during freezing weather.

Defining Property Boundaries

Many local building codes have specifications that boundary fences must meet. In many subdivisions, there are restrictions against using a tall fence to enclose a front yard. Local building codes should always be checked before building a boundary fence.

A good bet for those wanting a simple fence to define the front yard is a low post and rail or a picket fence. This type of fence is an effective way to discourage short-cutters, bicycle riders, and delivery men from cutting across the lawn. On the other hand, a low fence may look ineffectual and require nothing more than a high step or jump for someone to cut across the property.

LAWS AND REGULATIONS GOVERNING FENCES

Local ordinances and regulations regarding fence building are extremely variable from state to state and even from neighborhood to neighborhood. It is very important that you become familiar with these restrictions before building a fence.

There are regulations covering many different situations. Restrictions on barbed wire, electric wire, and other fencing materials of a hazardous nature are almost universal. There are also various ordinances limiting the height of fences near intersections. One community in the West permits a high fence if the portion higher than three feet is "composed of open work, such as chain link wire, wrought iron, lattice, or other suitable ornamental material and is constructed in such a manner that 80% of any portion is open to light and air." Another city limits the height of fences at intersections, but allows a homeowner to build a high fence if he designs it so that it is 35% open. Other areas have regulations covering such things as setback distance and the use of glass.

Sources of Information

The best source of information concerning restrictions is the community planning office (or zoning inspection department normally reached by contacting the city or county offices).

It is also a good idea to check the deed and title of your property to see if restrictions have been placed on it by previous owners. If you are employing a qualified fencing contractor, he should be familiar with state laws and local ordinances. Neighbors can also be helpful, but it is not safe to assume that a new fence is a proper one merely because it is similar to older existing fences in the neighborhood. New zoning ordinances may have been passed after the older fences were built. In cases where doubt exists, it is wise to seek competent advice before fence construction begins. A notice of violation is not a pleasant thing to find in your mailbox as it may involve an expensive and major alteration, or it may even call for removal of the fence.

A Fence May Be Required

Fence laws not only restrict and regulate the type of fence you build, but they may *require* you to erect a fence in certain situations. For example, many communities require protective fences around swimming pools, open wells, and excavations. Laws in other areas specifically state the height of a swimming pool fence, and call for special types of doors or gates. Property owners in rural communities are required to fence in all livestock except in open range country.

Who Is Responsible?

Problems can arise when the fence to be built is between adjoining landowners. Fences are generally considered as belonging to the land on which they are built, and a line or division-fence belongs to the neighboring property owners as tenants in common. An accurately surveyed boundary is necessary to assure that the fence is being put where it is intended to be .

It is desirable, if possible, to have an agreement with the adjoining landowner in advance, determining the location and type of fence and dividing up the responsibility for building and maintaining it. Such agreements, which should be in writing (for the sake of definiteness and in order to be binding under the laws of some states) can avoid many distressing disputes later on. They can be recorded in most states with the effect of fixing the responsibility for maintenance between future purchasers of the property.

Boundary fences erected by adjoining landowners together are usually placed on the property line, partly on the property of each, and are commonly owned. However, it is not always possible to secure the concurrence and aid of a neighbor in erecting a fence and in such cases it is advisable to place the fence entirely on the land of the builder, or a few inches inside the line to allow for possible errors in the survey. Such a fence is wholly the property of the landowner and he need not consult with his neighbor regarding its erection or maintenance as long as it does not violate any law, ordinance, or restrictive covenant.

Most states have laws to the effect that adjacent owners of "improved" or "enclosed" property are jointly obligated even without an agreement to bear the cost of erecting and maintaining line fences. If an adjoining owner chooses to let his land lie "unimproved" or "unenclosed" (depending upon the language of the particular statute), he need not contribute, but if he later on improves or encloses his land, he becomes obligated under the laws of some states to pay half the value of

---

HOW STEEP IS THAT RISE?

In laying out your fence, you will find it helpful to know exactly how steep a certain rise may be. There are many ways of determining this, but you can get a reasonably accurate idea by using a line level and a stretch of chalk line. Run the string from a stake at the high point in your fence line. Tie the string to the stake at ground level, and stretch it to a tall stake at the lowest point. Draw the string taut, hang the line level on the *center* of the string, and shift the string up or down on the tall stake as necessary until the bubble is centered. To be sure of an accurate reading, make certain that the twine does not touch anything— even blades of grass—and take measurements on a windless day. To calculate the drop, divide the height of the string above grade on the tall stake into the length of line between stakes.

---

fences built by his neighbors and assumes a share of subsequent maintenance costs. These laws are not uniform from state to state, and competent advice may be required to determine whether a legally enforceable obligation exists in particular instances. However, a landowner who improves his land after neighbors have fenced one or more sides will usually find it to his benefit to acquire an interest in these fences in order to have a voice in the manner in which they are maintained and in order to decorate his side as he chooses.

Division fences provide many opportunities for disputes. The solution of such disputes by force of law is not always satisfactory because neighbors must go on living next to each other afterward. A reasonable amount of cooperation in the erection and maintenance of fences for the mutual satisfaction of all can help neighbors avoid or settle most problems.

PLANNING FENCE LAYOUT

Before you get very far into your fence-building project, you should draw up a rough plan of the layout. It need not be very fancy or exact, but it should help you to estimate the materials you will need and to figure your way around any problems that you may have to solve along your fence line.

If every lot were as smooth as a baseball diamond, laying out a fence over its surface would be

CYPRESS TREES *form part of this grapestake fence; add to and relieve solid, vertical appearance.*

PALO VERDE TREE *was saved by incorporating it in board fence; fence was cut to fit tree contour.*

simple indeed. But few lots are so conveniently planned out. Often, the fence planner has to figure how to get his fence up a steep slope, across a stream, around a large tree. Problems such as these often call for professional solution, but here are some suggestions that may be helpful.

Avoid Existing Trees

Once in a while, erecting a fence is complicated by one or more trees growing right on the line where the fence should go. If the tree is small and doesn't fit into the garden plan, your best solution may be to remove it. However, if it is a large, handsome specimen that you want to preserve, you can incorporate it into the fence. Stop the fence an

inch or two short of the trunk, and be sure not to place the last post so close that you will injure the root system when you dig the post hole. The fence should also be designed so that its edge next to the tree can be "pruned" occasionally to accommodate the slow changes in the contour of the trunk.

Don't plan to include the tree in your fence line as a post. It can be done, but the practice is not to be encouraged. A tree is not likely to rupture the fence, for there is actually very little movement in the trunk of a large tree, even under severe wind stress. It will twist like a corkscrew, but it will not sway. The chief hazard in using the tree for a post is the possible injury that may be done to the tree itself. If you must attach anything to the trunk, be sparing in the use of nails. They break the outer skin of the trunk and permit disease and bacteria to enter. If too many nails are embedded in the bark or if wire mesh tends to restrict it or girdle it, the tree's sap flow may be stopped, with consequent injury or death. If lumber must be attached to the trunk, fasten it so it is held away from (and does not flatten) the bark.

On a Hillside Slope

If your fence line runs up hill, there are two accepted ways to lay out the fence: it may be built

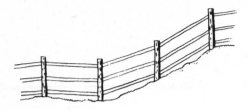

to follow the natural contours of the land or it may be laid out in steps. Some types of fencing adapt themselves easily to hillside contours, notably post and rail, and either rustic or milled pickets.

Less flexible are the more geometric forms, such as solid board, plywood, and louver. These can be canted to fit a hillside, but they require very careful cutting and fitting, and they look best if used in stepped sequence. Some suggested ways of using hillside fencing are shown in the illustrations below.

WIRED PICKETS are fitted to hillside contour. Solid board panels to one side act as separate planter.

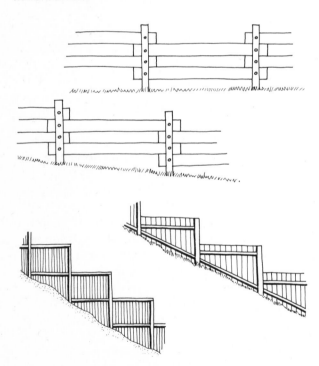

HILLSIDE FENCES follow varying slopes in geometric patterns, require careful planning for exact fitting.

Where Fences Cross Water

Much ingenuity is often required in constructing portions of fences that cross ditches, streams, or

BATTENED PANELS march down hillside in stepped sequence; separated rails at top add to design.

dry washes that flood in winter so that the fence will not create a barrier that will become choked with debris and either cause a neighborhood flood or carry away the fence.

One way to solve the problem is to install a floodgate: These are simple, rugged devices that open automatically at floodstage. A typical gate, as

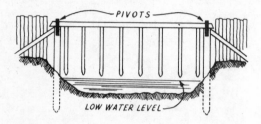

shown in the drawing, pivots on anchor posts on each side of the stream and swings upward as the water rises. Such a gate can also be slung on cables. Two vital requirements for sound design are strong anchor posts on each bank and provisions to prevent erosion of the bank, such as concrete side walls or a matte of saplings or wire. Gates should be cleaned out after every passage of flood water.

HORIZONTAL EFFECT of fence on sloping lot is achieved by concealing short boards at right with shrubs.

Design of floodgates is best entrusted to an engineer or landscape architect. (The "Farm Fences" booklet referred to on page 66 contains information on this subject.)

At the Edge of a Bank

When the fence has to be built along the edge of a stream or bluff, the fence layout should be worked out with an engineer or landscape architect as they will know just how close to the edge the fence can be put without losing it eventually to the wind or water action. Often, plantings along the bank will slow down the soil movement.

Rounding a Curve

If your fence plan calls for a curve, you can only secure a true arc by using some variety of railless (or palisade) fence, such as woven saplings or driven grapestakes. A slat fence can be built so it looks as if it were curved by bringing it around in a series of short chords. A curve in a wire fence under tension presents serious problems (see page 67).

Where to Get Design Help

In cases where you have a difficult engineering problem, or want advice on specific ways to fit your fencing program into an overall landscape design, you may want professional help. The cost of such aid will vary according to the kind of design help you choose and how much planning assistance you require.

The most complete and integrated solution is to hire a landscape architect to lay out the fence and the entire garden. He works much the same way as any other architect, submitting preliminary plans, and when one is approved, finished drawings and a planting list. Depending upon your agreement, he may also supervise the actual construction. Fees are usually based on a percentage of the complete installation costs.

Sometimes you can work with a landscape architect on a consultation basis, paying him by the hour. Under this arrangement he would help you with preliminary planning, then visit a couple of times during the installation process. Or you might work out a partial plan agreement whereby he designs and supplies plans for just the fencing at a specified fee.

A fence contractor is also often prepared to offer you low-cost design service, usually with the stipulation that you buy your materials from him and let him do a part of the installation. Of course, if you hire a contractor to do the entire job, you have the benefit of his engineering experience, and a reasonable assurance that he will install the fence to last, as well as correct any defects in construction.

Whether you choose a landscape architect or a contractor, it's a good idea to examine some of his previous work and talk with some of his former clients before you sign a contract. Don't be influenced by price alone—a poor job is no bargain at any price.

Highly paid professionals are not your only sources for design help. A city building inspector or county agent can usually tell you if your fence engineering is feasible, and often solves a few of your problems in the course of a routine inspection. The large national distributors of prefabricated fences will also provide detailed information and assistance (particularly if you buy your fence from them). Some of these firms will even provide you with a kit of all the tools you need to erect the fence.

For further information on fencing design and theory, see the companion *Sunset* book, *Landscaping for Western Living*.

WHO BUILDS IT?

Once you have chosen the type of fence best suited to your needs and its location, the question of who will build it must be considered. You can hire a fence contractor, do the work yourself (or with the help of a neighbor), or you can work in conjunction with the contractor. Here are some basic facts.

Hiring a Fence Contractor

There are several points in favor of having the fence completely built by a contractor. A fence contractor can put a fence in place much more rapidly than the weekend carpenter. The builder has access to specialized fence materials, preservatives, equipment, and experienced labor—a four-star combination that should produce sound results. If you choose a reputable builder, you can have confidence that the fence will be properly built, and if construction defects happen to show up later, you can be reasonably certain the contractor will correct them.

If you do arrange to have the work done for you, protect yourself (and the contractor) with a written contract. The agreement should specify grades of lumber to be used, types of preservative, if any, and other important details.

Building it Yourself

On the other hand, you may have persuasive reasons for attempting the task yourself. Perhaps finances alone rule out the hiring of a contractor, or perhaps you simply have the urge to create and build this addition to your property.

If you have a feeling for tools and a capacity for doing reasonably careful work, you should be able to erect a fence that is as sturdy and attractive as a professional job. Fence building is not one of the most difficult forms of carpentry. Materials are usually easy to obtain. Standard lengths of standard lumber can be used to build many types of fences, and materials for fences that require special trim or off-sizes can often be bought precut from lumber yards, mills, or fence dealers. Application of wood preservatives, which was once a messy and tedious task, has been simplified by the introduction of ready-to-use preservatives that can be applied successfully by soaking (see page 26-28).

If the fence runs along a property line, consult with your neighbor. Perhaps you can pool labor and divide material costs, or the two of you can combine resources to have the work done by a contractor.

Working With a Contractor

An alternative to doing the job yourself (or with your neighbors), or giving the whole job to a contractor, is to have the contractor dig the holes, set the posts, and leave the easy work for you. Unfortunately, though, this does not save as much effort and money as one might think. The time involved for a contractor to dig the post holes and set them so they are firmly embedded and precisely aligned represents a major portion of the fence building labor costs. Once the posts are up, the contractor can usually finish the fence quite rapidly. (It is always a good idea to ask the contractor for estimates of the job both ways to see if it is worthwhile to combine your efforts with his.)

TWENTY-TWO CHOICES OF FENCING

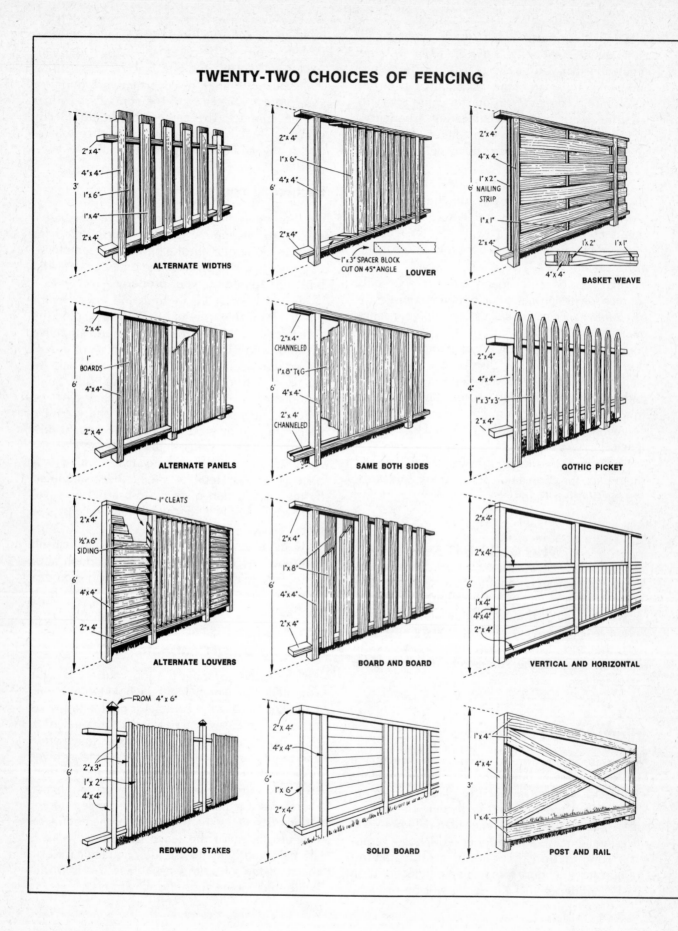

ALTERNATE WIDTHS

LOUVER

BASKET WEAVE

ALTERNATE PANELS

SAME BOTH SIDES

GOTHIC PICKET

ALTERNATE LOUVERS

BOARD AND BOARD

VERTICAL AND HORIZONTAL

REDWOOD STAKES

SOLID BOARD

POST AND RAIL

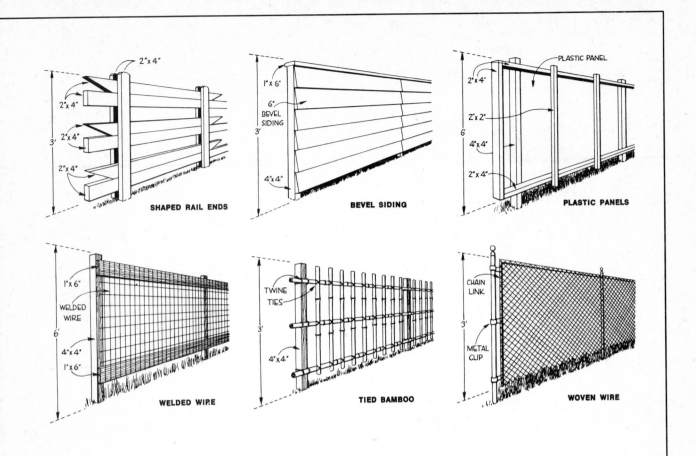

SHAPED RAIL ENDS

BEVEL SIDING

PLASTIC PANELS

WELDED WIRE

TIED BAMBOO

WOVEN WIRE

GRAPESTAKE FENCING VARIATIONS

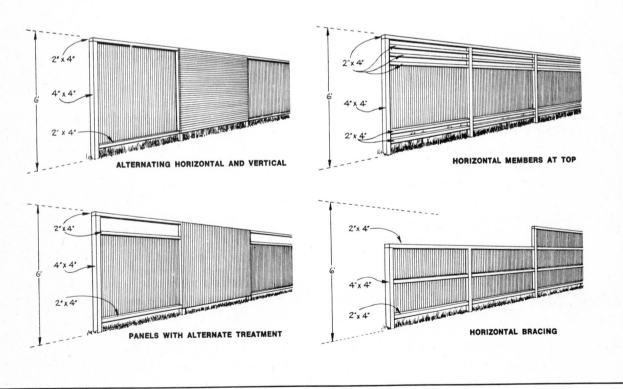

ALTERNATING HORIZONTAL AND VERTICAL

HORIZONTAL MEMBERS AT TOP

PANELS WITH ALTERNATE TREATMENT

HORIZONTAL BRACING

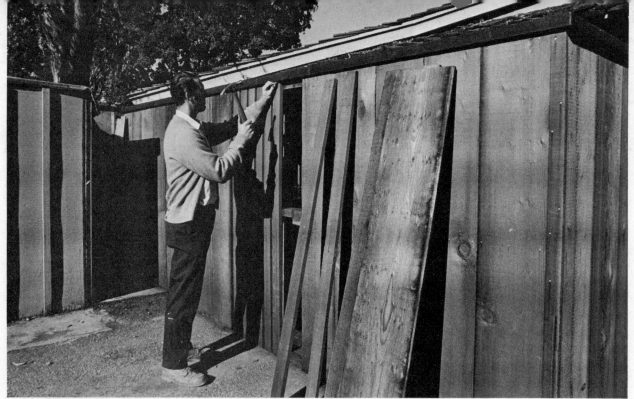

BOARDS *are easily attached to rails of wood fence.*

Building Fences and Screens

The actual process of fence construction varies with the type of fence that is being erected and the person who is building it. Some builders prefer to set all of the posts in place and then attach the other parts. This is normal procedure for fences that have butted rail joints (such as wire and woven picket fences) and for those that have their posts anchored in concrete.

As another variation, posts and rails can be put up at the same time where the rails and posts must be fitted together with an interlocking joint. If rails are joined in this way to concrete-anchored posts, it is important to attach them *before* the concrete hardens.

Other fence builders prefer to assemble the fence in sections, filling in the rails and pickets whenever two line posts are in place. This method is used for many of the prefabricated fences and for louver and board fences when sections are built on the ground and then lifted into place.

Fence building can be divided into three stages: the relatively easy, preliminary stage of plotting the fence; the more difficult stage involving exact alignment of the holes and of posts; and the third stage of adding the rails or stringers and siding. Each of these stages consists of a number of specific steps. Working within this framework, you can tailor the procedure to fit your specific situation.

PLOTTING THE FENCE

The first practical step in building your fence is plotting its exact course and marking the line with stakes and string. If the fence is located on or next to a boundary line, it is wise to have an engineer or surveyor lay out the corner stakes. Although such a survey will cost you a small fee, it will be much less than the later cost of shifting a sturdily built fence.

Of course, if your original survey stakes are still in place marking the boundaries of a newly surveyed lot, you might feel safe in using them for the fence line. Also, if the description of your property is exact enough in your deed, you might be able to measure out the lines yourself. However, if you do so, you would be wise to enlist the cooperation of your neighbors to avoid any possible misunderstanding. (If there are any remaining doubts concerning the location of the boundary in your mind, it might be a good idea to set the posts 6" inside the line just to be safe.)

Once you have established the end and corner points of your fence, the procedure is simple. You will need a long measuring tape, preferably steel; a carpenter's square; a ball of mason's twine, or any tightly-twisted string, such as discarded fishing line; some stakes; a hatchet; and a piece of colored chalk.

Here are the steps to follow:

1. Mark the end or corner points with a solidly driven stake, if each point is not already staked.

2. Run mason's twine between the stakes, draw it tight, and tie it firmly to the stakes. If bushes or other obstructions are in the way, use tall stakes so the twine will clear them.

3. Locate the sites for the remaining posts and mark with stakes. There are several ways to do this. You can simply lay the rails in line along the ground between the end stakes and drive in a stake wherever they butt against each other; or you can measure the intervals with your tape, either laying it along the ground or measuring along the stretched twine.

If you have a very long fence, like a country fence, you can plot its course by sighting stakes through a simple peep sight. Drive stakes (with tops painted white for better visibility) at either end of the planned fence line. Then make a peep sight by drilling a small hole in a board. Line up the end stakes by sighting them through the hole, and have a helper place the in-between stakes at your direction.

DIGGING, SETTING, AND ALIGNING THE POSTS

There are several accepted methods of digging post holes, setting the posts, and—what many consider to be the most difficult problem in building a fence—aligning the posts.

Digging Post Holes

The size of the post hole you dig depends upon the kind of soil, the height and weight of your fence, and the stresses it must withstand. If the fence is to be a wind barrier or an animal enclosure, it has to be stronger than ordinary boundary fence. Height is the primary consideration in determining how deep to set the posts. A good rule to follow is to sink posts at least $1/3$ of their length into the ground (thus you would use a 9-foot post for a 6-foot fence and sink 3 feet of it). Terminal posts (end, corner, and gate posts) need more support and are normally set deeper than line posts.

The bottom of the post hole should be wider than the top to provide a better, more solid base. Moisture should be able to drain past the bottom of the posts, so the hole should be 4 to 6 inches deeper than the posts will be set so that the bottom may be filled with rocks and gravel. You'll need an even larger hole in clay soil than in loose sandy soils. If posts are to be set in concrete, excavate $2^1/_2$ to 3 times the diameter of the post.

SPACING OF POSTS

Unless you are installing a prefabricated fence where you must work with a predetermined post spacing, you will probably want your posts to be evenly spaced. It is also a good idea to make the most economical use of standard lengths of rails (normally 2 by 4s). Normal residential fencing calls for spacing of not less than 6 feet or more than 9 feet between posts. Where it will work with your fence design, try to purchase rails at least twice the length of the post spacing. In this way you can nail the rails so that the ends fall on alternate posts (as illustrated), offering a much stronger fence.

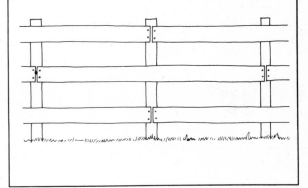

PLUMBING & BRACING THE POST

After the post hole is dug, shovel four to six inches of gravel into the hole and set the post on top of it. Then fill in as much gravel or soil around the post as is needed to hold it upright. Tamp the soil or gravel firmly while filling. Then true up the post by one of the following methods before filling in the remaining earth or concrete.

1. Check the two sides with a carpenter's level.

2. Check with a plumb bob. Suspend the bob from a string attached to a nail driven into a corner of the post, as shown in the drawing. By matching the bob line against the corner line from two directions, you can ascertain if the post is plumb in both directions.

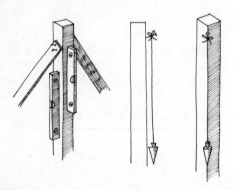

Once the post is plumbed, it should be braced to hold it temporarily in position while construction proceeds. Strengthen it with outrigger braces, one end nailed to the post, the other embedded in the soil and bolstered with a stake. Check the post alignment again, then fill in the hole with soil, gravel, or concrete (see below). Tamp the gravel solidly in place. Leave the braces attached until after the rails have been nailed on. The bracing will help the post to resist the shock of nailing.

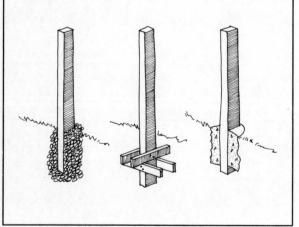

Setting The Posts

For a longer life, all fence posts should be treated with a wood preservative (see page 26) before setting them in place. There are several ways to set posts. In the case of a wire fence with steel posts, the posts can simply be driven into the ground. Wood posts can either be set in earth or gravel-filled holes, or for a stronger installation, in concrete. Described and illustrated below are the two most common methods of setting fence posts.

Setting posts in earth and gravel fill. Where the soil is stable (not subject to sliding, cracking, and frost heaving), backfilling with earth or earth and gravel works fine for most fence posts.

Dump a big base stone into each post hole, or use a few small stones or several inches of gravel. Tamp well, using a good-sized length of 2 by 4 lumber. Set in the post, and shovel in gravel a little at a time while you adjust the post until it's aligned and vertical. Continue filling with earth, earth and gravel, or gravel, tamping firmly every 2 or 3 inches. If the hole is wide, big rocks jammed

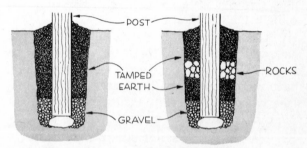

VIGOROUS TAMPING of earth is key to successful use of earth fill. Rocks near top help stabilize post.

around the post near the surface will minimize side movement. Slope the top of the fill so that water will run away from the post. In light, sandy soil—which offers easy shoveling but poor stability for fence posts—nail 1 by 4 cleats of heartwood cedar or redwood across the fence posts near ground level.

Setting posts in concrete. Concrete fill can use up a surprising amount of cement, sand, and gravel—but it gives the strongest setting by far. The concrete should be angled down at ground line to divert water away from the post. Don't let concrete get *under* the post, where it could hold in moisture and speed decay. *For this reason, never set fence post ends completely in concrete.*

For fence post setting in concrete, you can use a lean mix, with only a third the cement needed for a walkway mix. A mix of 1 part (by volume) cement, 3 parts sand, and 5 parts gravel is good. Keep the mix rather dry. To extend the mix, keep a supply of washed rocks on hand, and place them around the perimeter of the holes as you pour.

Using dry concrete mixes (cement, sand, and gravel all in one bag) saves ordering time and

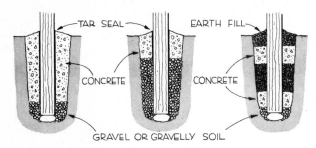

SETTING POSTS in concrete can be done three ways. For proper drainage, avoid getting concrete under posts.

trouble, and means you won't have leftover sand or gravel to dispose of. You will need about one bag of mix to pour around a 4-inch post, sunk 2 feet in about a 10-inch diameter hole.

Posts freshly set in concrete can be forced into a new position for perhaps 20 minutes after the pour; they should then be left alone for two days before boards or stringers are nailed on. During a spell of dry weather, fill the small crack between post and concrete with tar or caulking compound.

Frost heaving. Heavy frosts bring two problems: frost heaving, and concrete cracking. To minimize damage from heaving, dig post holes down to a foot below normal frost line; shovel in gravel; drive nails into the sides of each post near its bottom end, and place this end in gravel; pour

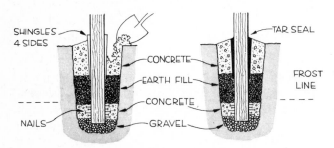

REMOVE SHINGLES after concrete has set. Pour tar between post and concrete to form expansion collar.

DIGGING TOOLS

Unless the residential fence builder has enough post holes to dig to justify the additional expense of power digging, or if his soil is extremely rocky, he usually must rely on hand tools and muscle. The two most popular digging tools are the auger and the two-handled clam-shell digger.

There are two types of augers—one is equipped with a screw blade and operates simply as a twist drill, the other has cutting blades combined with a scoop arrangement that holds the loose soil as it is bored out and also discourages the wall of the hole from caving in. Either type is best used in rock-free earth.

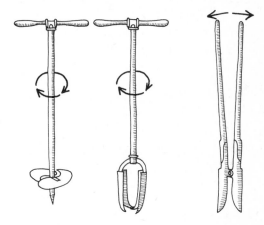

A two-handled clam-shell digger should be used in rocky soil. With this tool the fence builder plunges the blades into the soil and by working the handles back and forth chews his way down. It is difficult to use for digging a hole deeper than 2 feet, because the side walls interfere with the spreading of the handles. Working the handles back and forth also tends to break down the walls, producing a bigger and more ragged hole than needed.

In soil that is extremely rocky, a digging bar and a spoon-bladed shovel may be the only combination that will work.

If your fence requires a great number of post holes, and if the soil is not too rocky, power diggers are certainly worth investigation. Often you can contract the work to an expert with a specially rigged posthole-digger jeep. Also, some lumber dealers or fence contractors will lend you a digger if you buy your supplies from them. In some areas, one or two-man power augers are available in tool rental shops. A rented jackhammer equipped with a spading tip can also do the job.

concrete around nail area; complete the fill by using gravel or gravelly soil.

To prevent concrete collars from cracking when wet posts freeze and expand, cut shingles to width of posts, oil them, and place alongside each post before you pour. When concrete has set, remove the shingles and fill the open spaces with tar or sand.

Aligning the Posts

The most critical step in building a fence is aligning the posts. In order to achieve a handsome, straight and true fence, it is absolutely necessary that the posts be set plumb, are accurately aligned, and then solidly embedded so they will not lean with the weight of the fence.

To do a good job, you'll need a lot of patience, a good eye, a steady hand, and hopefully, a helper. You will also need a variety of tools: a carpenter's level, plumb bob, mason's twine, tamping bar (a 5-foot length of heavy pipe capped on one end will do), a heavy hammer, and some twenty penny nails.

There are several ways of coping with the problem of post alignment, and many experienced fence builders have developed their own particular methods. Described below are three of the most common and workable methods.

Corner post method. This is perhaps the easiest and simplest method to use. Begin with two corner posts. Set one permanently in place and fix the other one securely but not so firmly that it cannot be adjusted slightly. Or, you can set them both

LOCATE INTERMEDIATE POSTS by stretching strings between corner posts, transferring marks with a plumb.

permanently, exactly vertical (see special copy on how to set posts plumb) and with their faces in flat alignment. When they are in place, stretch aligning strings between them at both the top and bottom.

Mark points on the top line to indicate where the centers of the intermediate posts will be, and transfer the marks, using a plumb bob, to the lower line. Set each intermediate post in gravel, with its face brushing (but not distorting) the aligning strings. Backfill carefully, checking to see that each post remains vertical as you work.

If rough posts snag the aligning strings, slip a piece of ¼-inch material between each corner post and the strings, then nail it on. With batter boards move both ends of the cord ¼-inch. Then keep each intermediate post the same ¼-inch distance from the strings. Once all posts are in, make a final check by eye. (You can correct any misalignment at this time by pushing the post into the correct position and retamping the concrete or earth fill.)

Batter board method. With this method you plot fence post positions first and then set the posts successively. You can do this either with stakes which are set approximately three feet beyond each corner post or with batter boards (see sketch). Mark the intended post centers on the

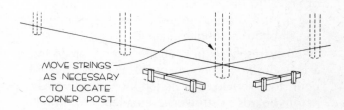

BATTER BOARD method uses string to position posts. Be sure to check vertical alignment of each post often.

aligning string. Continue as in the corner post method—but this time you will have only one string to guide you, and you'll need to check verticals frequently with a level or plumb line.

Here's a tip for plumb line users: Wrap the line around a piece of scrap wood half as thick as the bob is wide. Hold this block against any top corner of the post. When the plumb line lines up with the corner edge, and the bob is brushing the wood, the post is vertical.

One-man method. The "stake-out" method makes it possible for a man working alone to align a fence. Drive two stakes into firm ground near each post, as shown in the sketch, and nail an arm to each stake. Set posts onto rock or gravel at the bottom of the hole, checking alignment against the string. Use a level or a plumb bob to true one face of the post. Then tack its support arm in place. Do the same for the adjacent face. Check both

POUND STAKES at 90 degree angle to post and nail arm braces to stakes. Use level to check vertical.

verticals again, adjust the arms if necessary, and drive in the nails.

ADDING RAILS AND SIDING

Once the fence posts are up and firmly embedded, the hardest part of your fence building is over. The next step is to carefully attach the stringers or rails and siding (pickets, boards, grapestakes, or other materials) to the posts. If the stringers or rails are not attached firmly and squarely to the posts, all of your painstaking work in lining up the posts will be wasted.

Joining Rails to Posts

There are several accepted methods of fastening rails to posts, depending on the type of fence under construction and on the durability desired in the fence.

The first step, regardless of the method chosen for attaching the rails, is to apply paint or preservative to all surfaces where the rails and posts touch, for protection against decay. If paint is used, brush a generous coating of good quality base paint on both rail and post and attach the two while it is still wet. When the paint dries, it will seal the crevices. If the fence is to be left unpainted, coat the surfaces with a colorless wood preservative (see pages 26-28).

Lap joints. The simplest and commonest joint used in attaching rails is the lap joint. The rail is merely laid against or on top of the post and nailed in place. Top rails are commonly attached in this manner, even though the bottom rails may be attached by some other method. Rails lapped against the side of the post are not strong enough to support heavy weight, because most of the strain is carried by the nails. For this reason, rails attached this way are usually used only to carry light pickets or are used by themselves, as in a post and rail fence.

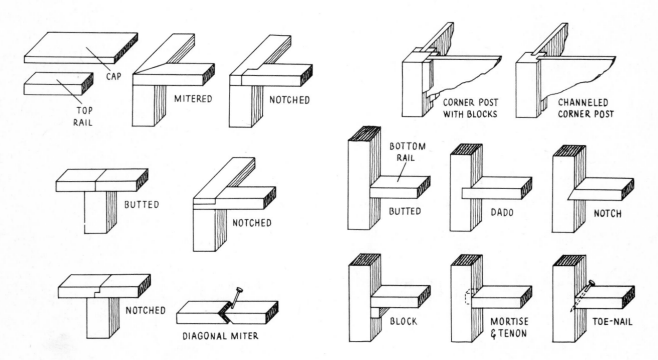

TYPES OF JOINTS which can be used in various fence constructions are shown here. Variations of four basic joints used by most carpenters are lap, butt, grooved, and mortised.

Butt joints. Another common fence joint is the butt joint. Rails are simply held against the post and toenailed in place. If the rails are wedged tightly between the posts, this type of joint is stronger than the lap joint because the posts help to support the end of the rail by friction. Rails attached this way can be used to support vertical boards, grapestakes, and heavy pickets. This joint is not recommended, however, for louver fencing.

Grooved joints. A more substantial joint is made by cutting a groove or "dado" into the post and fitting the rail into it. This type of joint is a good weightbearer and is used for bottom rails of louver or heavy board fences.

Mortised joints. Another strong joint can be formed by cutting a rectangular hole (or mortise) partly or all the way through the post and sliding the tip of the rail (tenon) into it. This joint is common in post and rail fencing, and it is frequently found in pre-built picket fences. It is clean, neat, and strong—but difficult for an amateur to fashion. If you plan to cut mortises in the posts, you will find it easier to work on them if you lay the posts flat on the ground. *Caution:* make sure that the bottom rail is level before setting the post permanently in place.

An imitation mortise and tenon joint can be easily assembled for a post and rail fence. The post is laminated of three layers of lighter wood, such as 1x4's to produce a 3x4 post, or 2x4's to produce a 6x4 post. The middle layer is omitted where the rail passes through the post, thus forming a mortise. Posts of this type are more likely to deteriorate than solid ones, because they are difficult to seal against moisture penetration.

Attaching Pickets, Boards, and Other Materials

Once you have finished installing your posts and rails, you will find the rest of the job is easy—but tedious. Attaching pickets is a simple operation, but if you have many to nail on, you will be very relieved to drive home the last nail in the last picket. For instance, in erecting a 100-foot stretch of grape stake fencing, you will drive more nails than you would to attach siding to a five-room house.

Before you attach the pickets, you should treat them with paint or wood preservative to protect them against decay in the same manner as you

treated the rails. As with the rails, attaching the pickets while the paint is wet will produce a more secure weather seal.

Uniform spacing. When pickets, slats, or boards are to be attached with an opening between each, here is a simple way to keep the spacing uniform: Cut a slat the exact width of the opening and attach a small cleat to one end. Hang it by the cleat on the rail alongside an attached picket, place the next picket against it, and nail the picket to the rail. Shift the cleat over one, and repeat (see sketch).

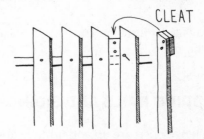

Pickets or boards placed snugly against each other will pull apart in time. If you desire a crackless fence, use tongue-and-groove, sleeved siding, or plywood sheeting.

Pickets should not be allowed to touch the soil; at least 2 inches clearance is advisable.

Painting

White is the traditional color for painted fences. It gives an appearance of neatness, complements floral display, calls attention to the fence in dim light, and sets a positive boundary line. Colored fences are frequently introduced as part of a garden design, to relate the fence to the house, brighten a wooded section of the property, liven up the play yard, or complement the floral color scheme.

Applying the paint. For long fence life, and infrequent repainting, use the best quality paints that you can obtain. For a superior finish, apply a base coat, and after it dries, brush on two coats of outdoor paint. You will find the application easier if you paint the pieces before they are assembled, as it is difficult to reach all parts and crevices with the brush after the fence is completed. When the fence is assembled, you can touch up hammer marks, hand prints, and nail heads.

Fences that resemble house siding, or those with large flat surfaces can be painted with an exterior type paint roller. There are rollers designed to paint in V-grooved siding and for corner work, though you may have to touch up a few spots with a brush.

Types of finishes. Your paint dealer can recommend the best finish for your particular climate and fence. If you are planning to plant against the fence, watch for mildew deposits; perhaps use a mildewcide in your finish. Remember that some garden sprays will stain painted finishes. Flush the fence with water immediately, if spray gets on the fence.

Caution: If white lead paint is applied to a fence that is penning in stock, the animals should be kept away from it while the paint is wet. Cows are fond of fresh paint and can lick off enough to get lead poisoning.

Casein is a very inexpensive water-based paint popularly used for painting fences. It is readily available in white and comes in 25-pound bags. Properly applied, top-quality casein is superior to whitewash, and can last as long as the more expensive water and oil-based paints.

Water-based latex paint is particularly good for fences, but it must be applied to a clean and relatively smooth surface. It cannot be applied to a previously painted fence which has oxidized or is cracking and peeling. Generally, latex lasts longer than any other paint—with the least amount of oxidation and fading of color. Latex made from an acrylic resin is usually considered to be the best.

On unpainted wood, two coats of exterior latex is generally all that is needed. However, if the wood is new red cedar or redwood, and you are using an off-white, a latex primer is needed before the exterior latex is applied.

A cleaning tip: Water-based paints can be washed from brushes and hands with water.

Standard oil-based paints are a good bet too, but they are messy to work with, and most fade and oxidize more rapidly than exterior latex.

Both semi-transparent and solid stains can be used on unfinished fences. Semi-transparent stains let some of the natural color of the wood show through, while solid stains color the wood and allow only natural grain and texture to be visible.

It is a good idea to choose a stain that contains varnish, creosote, or linseed oil. These stains will preserve the wood as well as color it.

Special stains have been developed for redwood that preserve its natural red color. On the other hand, a solution of baking soda and water (1 part soda to 10 parts water) will give redwood the grayish-black color that would naturally come with age. This solution will wear off within a year or two, but by this time the redwood will be darkening naturally.

Spray painting. Fences in the country are often spray painted, but this method is inadvisable (if not illegal) in the city. Wind can carry the paint droplets some distance and deposit them like permanent dew on neighbors' cars and windows. Furthermore, spray painting often does not give the lasting surface that a skillfully handled brush can provide, and the fence must therefore be repainted more frequently.

In skilled hands, however, a spray gun can quickly apply paint to fences that would be impossible to paint by hand, such as split rail, chain link, or 10-mile stretches of post and rail. Attachments have been developed that permit both sides of a fence to be sprayed simultaneously.

AN EASY WAY TO AGE REDWOOD

If you would like to give your redwood fence an aged look immediately, you can do so with common baking soda. Just mix ½ cup of baking soda with about a quart of water and brush or spray it on the wood, stirring the mixture often. As it dries, the acids in the redwood combine with the soda to produce a dark weathered tone. The baking soda does not darken other woods as effectively. And it will "weather out" of redwood in a year or two, but by then the natural darkening of the wood will have taken place. The mixture can be used on rough or smooth boards.

DARKENING EFFECT of baking soda and water solution is shown clearly on this sample redwood board.

PRESERVATIVES FOR WOOD

One of the disadvantages of using wood as a fence building material is that it is susceptible to decay. Decay is most likely to develop at points where the fence structure touches or enters the ground, wherever two pieces of wood fit tightly together, on surfaces where moisture can collect, or in joints where wood contacts wood or other construction materials.

The decay that shortens the life of a fence is caused by fungus growth. Whenever fungus spores (which are always present in the air and soil) find a comfortable environment in a fence post or joint, they give off a substance that literally dissolves the fibers in the wood, converting it into food for themselves. Fortunately, this process can be prevented or inhibited in various ways.

The simplest method for protecting wood (but the least effective) is to coat exposed surfaces with a good quality paint. This provides a protective skin that the fungus spores cannot penetrate. However, if this seal is broken at any point, or if it sloughs off, the spores get under the paint and go to work as enthusiastically as on unpainted wood. Paint has no protective value at all under ground.

Most woods not naturally resistant to fungus infestation can be provided with artificial immunity by chemical means. Wood preservatives, either soaked or forced under pressure into the wood fibers, will create an environment that is hostile to wood-destroying fungi and insects. Modern preservatives, properly applied, can make non-resistant woods, such as pine, cottonwood, and aspen, last as long or longer than the naturally more durable redwood and cedar heartwoods.

Wood preservatives can be divided into two classifications—those that are oil borne and those that are water borne. Among those that are water borne are the salt preservatives known chemically as Acid Copper Chromate (ACC), Ammoniacal Copper Arsenite (ACA), Chromated Copper Arsenate (CCA), Chromated Zinc Arsenate (CZA), and Fluor Chrome Phenol (FCAP), all of which are marketed under various trade names. These salt preservatives have much to recommend them over some of the older, better-known preparations. They are highly recommended, for example, where clean, odorless, and paintable wood is required.

However, for best effectiveness, the water-borne salt preservatives should be applied under pressure, a technique impossible for the homeowner. Also, the salts are poisonous to plant life and, being soluble in water, will leach out more readily than the oil-borne preservatives.

Best known in the oil-borne category is that granddaddy of preservatives, creosote. Two others popularly used are pentachlorophenol and copper naphthenate.

Creosote

Creosote solutions have been successfully used for decades to protect telephone poles, railroad ties, and fence posts. Creosote is long-lasting, insoluble in water, harmless to farm animals, and a very effective preservative if properly applied. However, it has some unpleasant traits that make it unpopular with many fence builders. The most obvious is creosote's heavy, medicinal odor, though this may not be a disadvantage in country fence installations. Principal objection to creosote is that once a post has been treated, the dressed area cannot be painted in a normal manner because the brown stain will quickly come through the paint.

The most practical way for the homeowner to apply creosote is to soak it into the post. A properly soaked post will last for a good many years, though not as long as if it were pressure-treated. Brushing creosote on the surface of wood to be buried in the soil does not do a satisfactory job, because the creosote does not soak deeply into the fibers of the wood.

Pentachlorophenol

Another preservative that has been recommended for decades is pentachlorophenol. It is a crystalline substance basically consisting of carbolic acid and chlorine which have been dissolved by solvents to make concentrated solutions. These concentrates are further diluted with either oil or gas for use in treatment. Pentachlorophenol can be obtained in concentrated solutions or diluted and ready-to-use. It also comes in two forms: ordinary pentachlorophenol and water-repellent "penta." In either form, it is popular with the homeowner because it is clean and practically odorless (oil-borne "penta" may have a slight petroleum odor, but this diminishes as the oils evaporate). Also, water-repellent "penta" is paintable.

The water-repellent pentachlorophenol, available under a variety of trade names, utilizes certain resins to make the wood almost completely resistant to water penetration. Once applied, the evaporation process starts immediately and leaves each tiny wood cell wall lined with a permanent elastic film. As a result, the cracking, swelling, and dimensional changes which normally take place as wood ages are fairly well controlled.

State colleges and forest laboratories call for a mixture of at least 5 per cent pentachlorophenol by weight for heavy-duty work. Preparations with less than this will not do the job where wood is in direct contact with the soil or close to it. Concentrated solutions are more economical, but it is more convenient to purchase the ready-to-use solutions unless you are treating a large number of posts such as on a country fence installation. The concentrates may be diluted with stove oil, diesel oil, or even crankcase drainings filtered through cheesecloth.

When applying pentachlorophenol, handle it with care and avoid undue exposure as it is highly irritative to the skin. Also avoid contact with plants in the garden—it has a secondary use as a weed-killer and will severely damage or kill a broad-leaf plant on contact.

Copper Naphthenate

Though more expensive than pentachlorophenol, copper naphthenate is favored by many home-owners—especially gardeners—because it is safe to use around plants. It is odorless and non-corrosive, but it stains the wood green, a major drawback where the natural appearance of the wood is important. It can be painted, but it normally takes two coats to cover. Copper naphthenate is also not soluble in water and will not leach out.

Hot Tar

Some fence builders advise dipping the ends of fence posts in molten tar, but forestry researchers caution against the practice. According to these authorities, the tar seal tends to trap moisture in the post and create an ideal environment for decay-producing fungi. Even if the post were perfectly dry when it was tar coated, it would eventually become damp as it absorbed rain water above the tar base.

A tar collar between the post and concrete footing is sometimes needed to protect the con-

crete against swelling of the post in freezing weather (see page 22). Also, it is not a good idea to set a post entirely in concrete as this may hasten decay (see page 20).

Precautions in Handling

Some wood preservatives can be severely injurious to the skin. Care must be taken to avoid direct contact with the material or splashing it into the eyes. For this reason, it's a good idea to wear goggles and rubber gloves while working with the material. Once the treated wood has dried, it does not present any hazard.

The petroleum solvents used in some preservatives are flammable, so they should not be handled near an open flame.

Applying Preservatives to Posts

The cold soak method for treating fence posts with preservatives is simple and inexpensive. Usually only the part of the post which will be below ground plus 6 inches of that which will extend above is treated. To further insure adequate protection, before the post is treated with a preservative, the surface may be pierced all around at whatever point the post will contact the soil level. This surface piercing breaks the outer vertical fibers and allows the preservative solution to soak in more deeply. The task is best done with a special implement, called an incising tool, which is similar to a single-bit Tennessee axe with two

rows of sharp teeth mounted on the back of the head (see illustration).

Ordinary 50-gallon oil drums can be used as containers for the treating solution. After 24 hours of soaking, a post will have an unbroken ring of treated wood, penetrating at least one-half to three-quarters of an inch.

Researchers have found that pine can absorb

the proper amount of pentachlorophenol for efficient preservation (4 to 5 pounds of preservative per cubic foot of wood) within 12 to 24 hours. Douglas fir, redwood, and incense cedar require a longer period—sometimes as long as a week.

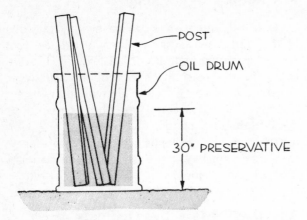

POST

OIL DRUM

30" PRESERVATIVE

Another method used on large scale commercial jobs is the hot bath treatment. Posts are placed in a hot treating solution which is then cooled, causing the air spaces within the wood to contract and draw in the preservative solution. (For detailed instructions on how to use this method, write to the University of California, Agricultural Extension Service, Berkeley, Calif. 94720, and ask for their booklet *Preservation Treatment for Grapestakes and Posts*.)

Applying Preservatives to Pickets and Rails

For long fence life, all parts that will be placed within a foot of the ground or exposed to dampness should be soaked in a preservative if at all possible. Where soaking is out of the question, paint the wood—literally sop it on—with a paint brush loaded with preservative solution. Pay particular attention to the ends of boards, where entry of moisture is most likely.

The ground stringer should be completely soaked from one end to the other. A long horizontal tub would be the best way to handle this.

The lower 6 inches of vertical boards should be soaked in the same manner as the posts. It might seem that the upper stringer could remain untreated; however, dampness is sure to gather at the ends, where the stringers join the posts. It is also a good idea to paint *every* joint with preservative after the fence is constructed. Be sure to apply additional preservative to all subsequently bored, sawed, or otherwise cut parts of treated portions.

Treat the exposed top surfaces of posts, too. This will prevent decay which results from standing water.

In the Northwest, and elsewhere where the year-round atmosphere is moist, it is best to soak completely *all* the wood pieces, for air-borne moisture can do as much damage as underground dampness.

RATING THE VARIOUS TREATMENTS

For best results, wood preservatives should be applied under pressure. This is simply because the effectiveness of the treatment depends upon the amount of preservative which is absorbed by the wood fibers, and much more fluid can be forced into the wood under pressure. The procedure requires large and expensive equipment, so it is usually done by a commercial firm. Most of these firms guarantee protection against decay for at least 25 years.

According to agricultural experts, the best home and farm methods for applying preservatives are as follows, in order of effectiveness:

Hot and cold bath. With this method, posts are thoroughly heated in a hot preservative solu-

tion and then put into a solution at normal air temperature. This requires two to four hours.

Hot bath. Only one tank is used for heating the oil and immersing the posts. The posts are then allowed to cool. This requires from four to eight hours.

Cold bath. The solution is used at normal air temperature. Most woods require soaking for periods from 24 hours to one week.

Experts do not recommend use of dipping, brushing, or spraying with most preservatives. However, some manufacturers claim that painting or spraying can get satisfactory results if the homeowner is patient enough to continue applying preservative until the wood absorbs no more.

FENCE MAINTENANCE

Even though you planned your fence carefully, and used the best materials for construction, it will require a certain amount of maintenance during its expected lifetime. Naturally, the better the fence is built, the less care it will require—but wind, rain, frost, wood-boring insects, rot, and fungus all take their toll of even the best quality fences.

A Fence Check-up In Spring

Spring is a good time to inspect the fence line for damage inflicted during the winter. If the rains have been heavy, the posts may be waterlogged and starting to decay. Examine them at the ground line for signs of rot, and dig away the soil to see how they are faring below the surface. If some decay is discernible, chip out the infected wood and drench the posts with a toxic wood preservative.

Check over the alignment of posts and pound down any that have been forced up by heaving of the soil due to frost action or drying of adobe clay. Drive in new nails where others have been worked loose by wind pressure on the boards, shifting of the post, or warping of the wood.

If the post has moved out of plumb, force it into line (an automobile jack is handy for this task), brace it straight, and tamp the soil down around the base. If the soil seems too unstable to hold the post, dig out around it and pour a concrete collar. If the slant of the posts is due to wind pressure, you may have to brace the fence on the weather side with guy wires or boards, or add small off-shoot fences to the lee side that will serve to brace the fence (and also add interest to your garden); or, if the fence is a solid-panel type, you may have to replace some of the air-tight panels with open-work to reduce the wind resistance. If your fence continues to lean after you have tried these remedies, you may have to devise some baffles to detour the wind currents away from the structure (see wind tests, page 8-9). If you reach this point, you should probably call for professional help.

Late spring is also a good time to check the plantings and miscellaneous vegetation alongside the fence. If a lush growth of weeds is seeking sanctuary from the hoe along the fence, turn them under or spray them with a toxicant and form a firebreak. Inspect vines and climbing roses growing beside the fence for tendrils that have worked themselves into the fence joints where they will

pry it apart. Prune plantings where they rub against galvanized fencing so they will not corrode the zinc plating off the wire.

If paint has started to blister or flake away, brush it clean with a wire brush and repaint. Paint should be applied as often as the house needs it—usually once every 3 to 5 years.

Repair or Replace Rotted Posts Early

It is best to repair or replace rotting posts before they rot completely through. When a post loses its structural strength because of rot, it not only fails to hold up its share of the fence but it adds its own weight to the increased weight the neighboring posts must support. Deterioration of a whole section of the fence can proceed rapidly when this point is passed.

If a post rots away at the ground level, there are three ways of repairing it: it can be replaced with a new one set in place a foot or so away; a

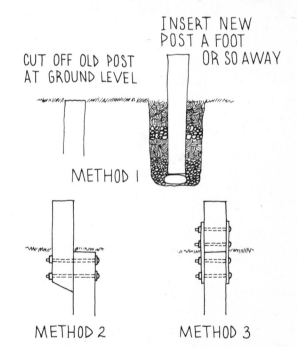

new section can be set in alongside the old one and attached to the top of the old one; or the rotted section of the post can be sawed out and steel braces bolted to the top and bottom parts of the original post.

If it is necessary to remove a sound, whole post, you will need mechanical assistance. To extract a post from the soil takes a great deal of leverage. This can be supplied by a post puller that you can buy or rent in some localities.

POST AND RAIL is classic favorite among wood fences.

Wood Fences – the All-Time Favorites

Of all the materials available today, wood remains the most commonly used item in fence and screen construction. Its versatility, availability, and ease of handling make it a favorite with most fence builders. Other materials are almost always used in combination with wood (one exception is the all-metal fence—see page 63).

Within the spectrum of wood fences, the most popular are board, grapestake, louver, and rail. Architects and imaginative homeowners have come up with several fresh new approaches to these basic styles, which will be examined in this chapter.

Because of increasing costs of materials and labor, the general trend in fencing is toward simplicity of style and use of the lower wood grades. For example, the original grapestakes were approximately 2 by 2 inches, now they are almost always 1 by 2 inches. Whereas fence posts were often quite large, dealers report that they now almost never get requests for posts larger than 4 by 4 inches.

Prefabricated wood fences are also growing in popularity. These fences can be ordered in a wide variety of styles from lumber dealers, fence contractors, directly from the factory, and from large chain stores. Prefabricated fences usually come in complete, ready-to-assemble kits—including posts, rails, pickets or panels of surfacing material, nails, and complete instructions for assembling.

There are many sizes, shapes, and styles of wood fences. Most, however, are variations on one of about 12 basic styles. In this chapter these basic styles are grouped into two broad physical categories: *low fences* (up to four feet) and *high fences* (four feet and higher). There is, of course, some overlap, such as the grapestake fence which can be used effectively as both high and low fencing.

LOW WOOD FENCES

If you desire a boundary fence which will not obstruct a view or one that will add to the appearance of your property, consider any one of the low wood fences discussed below and on the following pages.

The Picket Fence

The militant line of a picket fence will define a property line exactly and emphatically yet its low height and the openness of its structure does not present the forbidding look of "no trespassing." Traditionally, the picket fence has been associated with Colonial architecture, but today it is found paired off with almost any type of house, whether located in the city or in the country. The typical picket fence is about three feet high and has three-inch Gothic pickets spaced three inches apart.

In recent years, ready-made pickets have become increasingly difficult to find. Those lumber dealers who carry ready-made pickets offer a limited choice. Other dealers will cut the pickets

from standard lumber stock only upon request. Homeowners who want pickets with complex top designs normally end up doing the cutting themselves.

Despite the scarcity of ready-made pickets, landscapes continue to be dotted with a variety of picket fences. Much of the effectiveness of picket fence design is due to its repetitive quality, but in

a long stretch of fence, this can become monotonous. There are various ways of introducing some variety into the pattern: use tapered pickets (slightly narrower at the top) to provide a subtle change; mix different width pickets together, alternating wide and narrow; or alternate pickets of different heights.

The Rail Fence

A direct descendant of the pioneer's fence, the rail fence is simply constructed of the two basic components of a fence—posts and connecting rails. (An exception would be the palisade fence, constructed entirely of stakes or posts with no connecting rails. See examples of this on pages 13 and 48.)

The most venerable of the rail fences is the picturesque zigzag (also known in the early days as the worm, the snake, and the Virginia rail fence). This fence was almost universally adopted by early settlers when wood was plentiful and the rails were a by-product of clearing heavily timbered lands. In those days boundary lines were flexible enough to take a broad gauge fence. The rails were about eleven feet long, and laid at an angle so that each section formed eight feet of the fence line. The base width was about five feet (for stability), and the height varied from five to eleven rails.

When timber and land started to become more valuable, the kinks began to disappear from the rail fence. As timber became even more market-

TRIM AND FRIENDLY, this picket fence has pointed post caps to emphasize the basic picket design.

PICKET TOPS have an unlimited range of designs; doughnut-shaped top shown here was specially cut.

ARROWHEAD DESIGN for redwood picket tops is suitable for setting; posts are attached to concrete base.

ROUND, TAPERED PICKETS give fence an elegant, formal look. Cap on end posts emphasizes top design.

CLOSELY SPACED, these subtly shaped pickets present a softer, less severe appearance than other designs.

COLONIAL ATMOSPHERE of this early Monterey-style house is enhanced by crisp dart-shaped picket fence.

CIRCLE-SHAPED TOPS give this picket fence a whimsical look; corner post is base for entry lamp.

ZIGZAG RAIL was forerunner of today's rail fences, was commonly built when timber was plentiful.

RAILS STRAIGHTENED out in this manner when lumber became scarcer and property lines were more exact.

FEWER RAILS used even less lumber and today's post and rail fences usually have only three or four rails.

POST AND BOARD using dressed lumber replaced fence with split rails, has become well known favorite.

able, the fence began to shed rails, finally arriving at the two and three-rail variety that is popular today.

A shift from split rails to sawn lumber, from post and rail to post and board, ended the evolution of the rail fence. This conversion was inevitable because dressed lumber became much more common to the fence builder than raw timber.

The rail fence is ideally suited to the country scene. Its horizontal lines gracefully follow either rolling or flat terrain. It is economical in lumber usage, particularly if it is built of raw materials near at hand. A sturdy rail fence is a strong enough barrier for containing cattle and horses.

Some varieties of rail fences fit easily into urban landscaping. Light rail fences go best with ranch style homes but look well with many other styles. One or two-rail post-and-board or low split-rail

fences often make good boundary fences for the front yard. They discourage short-cutters but don't block the view or shut off sunlight from plants.

Rail fences are generally less expensive than picket or board fences. Some of them are the simplest of all fences to build, requiring only casual workmanship. The more sophisticated varieties, with fitted mortise and tenon joints, do call for more painstaking work.

The zigzag fence is not frequently built these days because of the lumber it requires (though many old ones can still be seen in the country). Where there is a surplus of timber, a rustic zigzag fence can be put together fairly easily. Usually split rails or second-year growth is used. The fence can be assembled by setting double posts where the rails cross; splitting and interlocking the ends of each rail; or driving dowels or steel pins through

SPLIT RAIL CONSTRUCTION is not difficult. Rails are stacked between posts and fastened with wire.

TOP RAIL is set at angle to prevent children from walking fence and to protect post tops from rain.

the rails. If heavy wood is used, the weight of the rails will hold the fence without additional support.

Split rail fence. In the split rail fence, the rails are laid one on top of the other and held in line by posts set in pairs alongside the overlapping ends. It can be built with rails of any size and weight, but its most popular Western form is fashioned with grapestakes.

The horizontal grapestake is inexpensive, requires no upkeep, and is easy to build. It is found in various heights, ranging from a miniature fence two or three rails high for rimming a flower bed, to standard-height fences for enclosing a vegetable garden or an orchard. This fence is not sturdy (it will not withstand climbing children, and it will not exclude some animals).

Construction of the split rail fence is simple. First, lay out the fence line as described on page 18. The distance between posts should be a foot or so shorter than the length of the rails to allow for overlap at each end. Set the paired posts in holes or drive them into the ground. Place them the width of a rail apart (using a rail as a spacer gauge). Set all the posts before stacking the rails in line. Attach the rails to the posts with galvanized wire, twisted tight, or with nails driven through the posts.

Post and rail fence. A handsome and long-lasting fence, the old-fashioned post and rail is still very popular in many areas for enclosing stock pens, fields, orchards; or for giving a decorative border to a ranch type home. It requires little maintenance because there are no spikes or wires to rust and work loose.

Posts are made from round peeled lengths of timber, 6 to 8 inches in diameter. They are set up to $2\frac{1}{2}$ feet into the ground, to provide staunch support for the rails. Mortises are cut all the way through the posts to hold the rails, which are tapered to wedge inside. Rails normally consist of long poles cut from second or third-year growth.

Posts are customarily placed 10 feet apart. This long span requires that the rails used must be strong enough to support their own weight without sagging.

Construction calls for some skill in handling tools. Rail ends are commonly shaped with an axe or draw knife, mortises are bored out with a large auger and then smoothed with a chisel. It is rough work, for the posts and poles are quite heavy to handle.

Those wanting to avoid the carpentry phases of erecting a post and rail, can buy the fence materials already shaped to fit. Well-made, natural-looking prefabricated post and rail fences are obtainable from dealers.

To set up this fence, dig the post holes, plant the first post; fit the rails into the mortises, and then set the next post in its hole. Fit the other ends of the rails into the second post, tamp it firmly in place; then wedge in the next set of rails, and continue in this sequence around the fence line.

Post and board fence. The post and board fence is the direct descendant of the post and rail. It is basically the same fence, but built with dressed lumber instead of hand-hewn timber.

The typical post and board fence is 3 to 4 feet high and has three rails. Two and four-rail types are also common. Rails are set varying distances apart. If the fence is to be used for penning stock, rails are spaced closely enough to keep a horse or cow from poking its head through.

Posts should be heavy-duty, at least 6x6 inches, and they should be sunk in the ground at least 2½ feet.

There are two main types of post-and-board fencing. With one, the rails are let into mortises in the posts in imitation of the old-style post-and-rail. With the other, boards are nailed to the sides of the posts.

Mortised rails. Posts are mortised to take rail tenons (see page 23) in one of two ways: a broad mortise lets the rails overlap side by side; a long, narrow mortise lets them overlap one above the other. When rails overlap at the side, a very wide and heavy post is needed, but this joint adjusts more easily to sharp changes in grade than a joint with one rail above the other.

Span between posts may be 8 to 12 feet, depending on the weight of the rail (2x4, 1x6, etc.). Posts may be solid or made of three or four layers of lighter wood.

Lapped joints. When the rails are attached to the sides of the posts, lighter weight boards are usually used for rails and the span between posts is reduced to 8 feet. The two favorite boards for this fence are 1x6's and 1x8's.

The top rail is often attached with a slant. This makes the fence look sturdy, prevents children from walking along it, and protects the tops of the posts from rain. One problem is that rails attached at an angle will eventually sag.

RAILS ARE MORTISED to posts which are shaped to shed rainwater and forestall possible decay.

BATTEN ON POST (foreground) adds to fence appearance and design strengthens the board ends.

CURVED PANELS of pickets cut to different lengths is one way to introduce variety into this old favorite.

MIDDLE RAIL is smaller in variation of the post and board. Note that top rail is inset, other butted.

VINE-COVERED grapestake pickets bring a touch of the country to streetside yard of this city residence.

ENCRUSTED WITH MOSS, the venerable grapestake fence is a familiar sight along many country roads.

ROSES AND PICKETS have long been a compatible two-some; heavier vines require pruning to prevent damage.

RAGGED TOPS of grapestakes give a casual appearance to this low, informal fence.

LOW BOARD FENCE utilizes sections of telephone poles for posts which are grooved for attaching rails.

HAND SPLIT RAILS produce a sturdy and long lasting fence which requires very little or no upkeep.

CLOSED POST AND BOARD variation substitutes slats for middle rails; prevents wanderings of children, pets.

LATTICE PATTERN post and rail looks trim and orderly on top of red brick wall. Posts and rails are 2 by 2's.

DIAMOND-SHAPED BRACING in post and rail fence adds strength as well as beauty, does not block view.

HIGH WOOD FENCES

Homeowners desiring a more protective fence will choose one of the high fences. Most of the fences in this category lend themselves more to privacy, security, and control of the environment than do low fences. A great many of the fences described below can be built in low models, but they are most commonly found in their higher forms.

The Grapestake Fence

This truly Western fence is built with redwood stakes—unchanged in design from those that have been used for generations in vineyards to support grape vines. Perhaps the most versatile of the wood fence materials, grapestakes can be used vertically or horizontally in both high and low fences. They can make a rugged fence when used as uneven pickets or they can take on a formal air when enclosed within a frame.

Grapestakes are about 2 inches square, and 3 to 6 feet in length. Because they are split from redwood logs, they have irregular, splintery edges. They were originally split from heartwood, but there is a trend today toward the use of sapwood. Often, too, they are sawed in half lengthwise to form 1x2-inch pickets with one rough side and one flat side for easier nailing.

Grapestakes are popular for several reasons. Because redwood is more decay resistant than most other woods, fence maintenance is low.

Also, the lightweight stakes are easy to handle and install. Another good quality of grapestakes is their appearance. Natural reddish in tone to start with, they weather to a soft, silvery gray that blends smoothly with plantings, and complements the warm tones of brick and stonework in the garden.

An often heard criticism of grapestake fencing is that it has been used too indiscriminately and that too many miles of stakes have been erected in some areas. Some homeowners object mainly to the rough splintery surface. Others are deterred by the inevitable weathered gray appearance and the cost (they are not cheap).

Grapestakes are adaptable to several different methods of construction. Often they are nailed like pickets to a fence frame (pointed tip up for a rustic effect, or squared tip up for a clean fence line). They may also be fitted inside the frame to provide a two-sided fence or attached vertically, horizontally, or in alternating panels to produce interesting patterns. They may even be driven directly into the soil.

The Slat Fence

Strips of rough finished redwood or cedar are customarily used to build the slat fence. It is not limited in height, since the 1x1 or 1x2-inch slats are cut from standard lumber; therefore, it is often used for tall screening. Slat fences are more formal and tailored looking than the splintery grapestakes and look more at home in a city environment.

VERSATILITY OF GRAPESTAKE FENCING is shown here in the rugged, informal screen at left and in the formal and tailored barrier at right. Both are good backdrops for a variety of plantings.

Slats can be nailed over a frame like grape-stakes, and they can either be set close together or spaced. They can also be overlaid on a solid fence to create interest on a plain surface. Their straight, clean lines are particularly effective for creating a strong, vertical pattern.

Slat fences are particularly helpful in controlling wind problems. Wind tunnel tests indicate that open slat fences often provide more effective wind protection than most other types of fences.

The Louver Fence

This fence is handsome and useful, but it is quite expensive to construct.

By adjusting the angle of the louvers, the fence can be used to control several factors. By orienting them to the path of the sun, maximum light and shade can be furnished for plants. If they are faced across the path of prevailing winds, air circulation can be tempered in a garden. By setting them with their "blind" side toward the public, they can screen off a service area without restricting the flow of air.

Narrow louvered panels can also be placed near entryways or front windows to permit the householder to view the street or entry walk, but prevent the passerby from looking in.

Vertically placed louvers provide only "progressive privacy," that is, some part of the garden is fully visible through the fence as a person moves along it. To secure absolute privacy, horizontal louvers are required. But while these will provide a more effective screen, they are subject to structural weaknesses that discourage many builders from using them.

Louver fences are strong in design. The pattern of alternating strips of shadow and highlight, varying through the day as the sun's angle changes, provides an interesting feature in the garden. Louver fences are meant to be seen and consequently have to be carefully worked into the landscaping plan. They should not be concealed under vines or hidden behind shrubs. Over-planting along the fence line will close off the view and interfere with the flow of air through the louvers.

Because of its architectural quality, louvered fencing should be matched to the design of the house itself. It is often treated as a part of the house, or as a means of tying to the house some element that is half-house, half-outdoors, such as a carport or an outdoor room. If painted or stained the same color as the house, or a tone that complements it, this relationship can be further strengthened. Although louvered fencing can be used with most styles of residential architecture, it appears least conspicuous when used with modern-type structures that utilize simple planes, angles, and shadows to achieve their exterior lines.

Construction costs can be high. The principal faults of the louver fence are its high construction costs and certain inborn weaknesses. The two are related, because much of the expense involved in

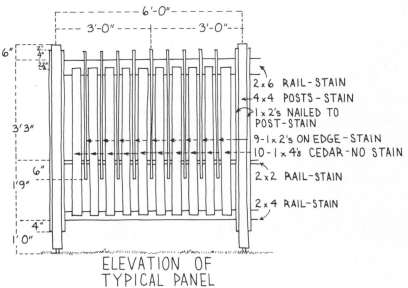

ELEVATION OF TYPICAL PANEL

2x6 RAIL-STAIN
4x4 POSTS-STAIN
1x2's NAILED TO POST-STAIN
9-1x2's ON EDGE-STAIN
10-1x4's CEDAR-NO STAIN
2x2 RAIL-STAIN
2x4 RAIL-STAIN

SHADOW PATTERNS which result from alternating a flat board with an on-edge board as shown in the drawing produce an interesting screen. Variation in photo alternates two flat and two on-edge.

ROUGH GRAPESTAKES, alternating flush and recessed panels in darker framework, enclose a country pool.

STAINED WHITE grapestakes have neater appearance than unfinished lumber. Green vines provide contrast.

HAND CHIPPED redwood slats give unusual and interesting texture to fence set in tropical plantings.

VARIED SPACING of slat fence gives desired privacy (foreground), lets in light and view (rear).

FRAMESIDE VIEW shows sturdy construction of this grapestake fence; bottom rail on edge adds strength.

LATH SCREEN gives entryway light and air, blocks view of busy street. Wood varies in width, thickness.

VERTICAL SLAT provides tall, curving garden screen. Strips are spaced slightly apart for progressive privacy.

VERTICAL LOUVER next to board and board was solution to neighbors' different tastes in fence design.

ENTRY COURT SCREEN is made of 1 by 1 slats spaced 1/2 inch apart. Screen and framing are dark brown.

SLANTED LOUVER FENCE is attractive, but unless built of kiln dried lumber the louvers will sag.

ADJUSTABLE LOUVERS can be closed for weather protection, opened to add light or to capture a breeze.

RIGHT ANGLE LOUVERS, 1 inch thick, contrast with vertical lines of brick wall; metal brackets hold posts.

WIDE AND NARROW BOARDS, alternately spaced an inch apart, relieve stark appearance of solid board fence.

A-SHAPED CAP protects board fence during rainy season, enhances structural design of house beyond.

erecting such a fence is due to the extra costs in premium lumber and careful workmanship needed to prevent the fence from deteriorating.

Several factors force the costs upward. In the first place, louver fencing requires a larger amount of material than any other wooden fence. More vertical boards are required per running foot than for a solid board fence of comparable height. Secondly, the louvers are supported only at the ends without center bracing, and this tends to encourage them to warp and twist after several months' exposure to sun and rain. To prevent this, many fence builders use top-grade (and top-price) kiln-dried lumber, and apply some variety of moisture seal. If the louvers are installed horizontally, they are sure to develop a sag unless the span between the posts is fairly short or the boards are supported in the middle.

Another complication is due to the heavy weight of the fence structure. Much of the weight of the louvers is borne by the bottom rail, which may sag and throw the framing out of alignment. Because of this, the whole structure requires strong posts and substantial foundations.

Finally, louver fences consume a surprising quantity of paint, because of the unusually large surface area that must be covered.

Because of all these reasons, louver fencing is usually found in fairly short installations, placed expertly where fullest advantage of its features can best be obtained.

The Board Fence

There is an almost unlimited range of designs and variations of board fences. These fences are useful and easily built, but they must be carefully, thoughtfully designed and placed to overcome a formidable array of disadvantages. Solid board fences are expensive, because they require a large amount of lumber. They give maximum privacy, but too often at the expense of creating a boxed-in feeling. The blank surface can be monotonous and cheerless, and in many of its variations, the board fence has a definite wrong side that either the homeowner or his neighbor must look at.

But the disadvantages which force thoughtful design often result in a fence that is tailored to a specific role, and which performs this role more efficiently than any other fence.

Variation relieves solid appearance. Board fences can be given interest and pattern through any number of variations.

At a sacrifice of some privacy, all tall board fences may be opened up slightly to produce a lighter feeling and a hint of the world outside. Boards may be set slightly separated like pickets, or they may be placed slantwise within the frame to form a louvered fence (discussed on pages 39 and 42). The upper quarter of the fence may be left open or fitted with an inset of lattice or open-spaced slats.

The blank surface area can be broken up by using materials that give pattern or texture to the structure, such as board and batten, siding, or tongue and groove; or by alternating panels with vertical and horizontal boards; or by varying the direction of the fence, using a zigzag or serrated fence line.

Horizontal siding will give the fence a strong horizontal feeling and appear to stretch a small garden; vertical siding will seem to compress a long fence.

The right-side wrong-side problem can be solved by designing the frame side so it has strong interest in itself, or by fitting the boards wholly within the frame so the fence appears the same from both sides. The frame side can also be improved with a simple trellis that will fill in with colorful vines.

A solid fence can be treated as an integral part of the house plan. Designed as an extension of the house wall to enclose the outdoor living area, it gives a feeling of continuity to outdoor-indoor living within its enclosure. Viewed through a glass wall, it becomes an outer wall of the house itself. The inner surface should therefore be finished in materials that harmonize with interior wall materials and color schemes. The public side of the fence should be surfaced with the same materials as the house—siding, shakes, board and batten.

Board and board variation. One of the most popular variations of a board fence is the board and board, also known as the shadow fence. This fence offers some of the advantages of the louver fence, but it is easier and less costly to build.

Boards are nailed to the frame with an open space slightly narrower than the board left between them. Another set is then nailed to the other side, with the open spaces opposite the boards on the first side. The fence is thus the same on both sides.

The baffle-like arrangement of the boards breaks up strong wind currents but allows air to circulate freely. Like louvers, when the boards are placed vertically, they give filtered privacy and light; when they are set horizontally, they give absolute privacy, but pass no direct sunlight. This fence also takes on interesting shadow patterns as the sun advances, in contrast to straight board fencing.

One great advantage: this fence can be assembled with mediocre lumber, because a small amount of warping is not noticeable with this design. Some homeowners feel that this advantage is overshadowed by the limited value the fence offers in security. Small animals can wiggle their way through either vertical or horizontal panels, and the horizontal variety offers an attractive climbing surface for children and intruders.

VERTICAL BOARD AND BOARD gives less privacy but is harder for children to climb than horizontal variety.

SOLID BOARD fence provides maximum privacy. Plantings soften the big, wall-like expanse of lumber.

VERTICAL BASKET WEAVE has slat centers woven around center rail, ends crisscrossed to top, bottom rails.

WOVEN PATTERN of basket weave can have dizzying effect. Here espaliered pyracantha helps soften it.

CLOSELY WOVEN variation of basket weave uses strips of cigar box thickness in a tight, diagonal pattern.

The Basket Weave Fence

Basket weave fencing is well known for the minimum amount of materials it takes to create an almost solid screen. Other good qualities are its interwoven design (which makes it surprisingly strong for its weight) and the attractive appearance it offers on both sides.

Some people, however, find the weave unattractive and dizzying when used in long stretches. Others object to the unsubstantial, almost shabby look some installations attain in a surprisingly short time. The basket weave is also extremely difficult to paint after it is erected.

There are many variations of design possible with basket weave. It can be horizontal or vertical, and the weave can vary from flat to very wide and open. One version uses very thin, lightweight strips, crisscrossed in a tight weave.

There is a simpler version of the basket weave that is not a "good neighbor" fence. Boards are nailed on the same side of the posts and then "woven" into the basket weave pattern by inserting spacers from the top on alternate sides of the boards. This type of fence is usually finished off with the addition of a top rail.

Lattice and Treillage

Strictly speaking, the term lattice should refer to structures built of thin lath, but it can be applied to a wide variety of grid-like screens, fences, and treillage, whether constructed of heavy or light lumber.

Lattice fences can be used for several purposes in the garden. A tightly woven lattice can be used to screen out an objectionable view, or to shield a service yard or garden work center. With its spaces opened wide, a lattice will let in a view, serve as a traffic director, or double as a display tier for potted plants.

Lattices may be used to support climbing roses and other vines. However, such plantings must be kept pruned or they will run away with the fence. They also have to be removed to permit periodic repainting. As some vines damage wood by keeping it too damp, it is wise to check with your nurseryman before planting alongside a lattice fence.

Also used to liven up the blankness of a solid wall, lattice work should be fastened on so it can be removed or lowered at repainting time.

Treillage is usually associated with Victorian architecture. Traditional, elegant, and lacy, trelliswork can be very decorative in applications ranging from statue niches or arbors to summer houses.

Construction of treillage requires painstaking attention to detail and the best of architectural design because it must appear light and airy and yet be strongly constructed. It is often best to have it installed by an expert craftsman.

Solid Wood Panel Fences

There is a wide variety of sizes, styles, patterns, and textures of exterior plywood and hardboard now on the market which are adaptable to fences. Fences built of solid wood panels offer some distinct advantages: The fence goes up very quickly, particularly if post modules match the panel size; the flat planes make good display surfaces; and the panels insure complete privacy. On the negative side, consider these drawbacks: The panels require strong structural support, especially in windy locations; a long panel fence often seems confining; and some of the materials have a tendency to weather and warp.

Here is a brief rundown on the panel materials:

Plywood. An old standby for solid panels, plywood comes in several thicknesses, standard widths of 4 feet, and lengths from 6 to 10 feet. Surface types available in exterior grade (for fencing) include rough sawn, grooved, channeled, and lapped. You can purchase plywood that is unfinished, primed for painting, or pre-stained in a variety of colors.

There have been attempts to improve the durability of outdoor plywood by protecting it from excessive weathering, warping, cracking, and buckling. One type of panel that shows some promise has shallow, closely spaced striations cut vertically to relieve the surface tensions which develop in the face of the veneer. These striations are not highly visible from a distance, and if desired, can be worked interestingly into the elements of the fence and yard.

A new plywood product, with fairly limited applications in fencing, has a surface of stone aggregate (applied with epoxy) in a variety of textures and colors. These panels are available in sizes of 4 feet by 8, 9, or 10 feet.

Hardboard. Made of wood fiber that is bonded under heat and pressure, hardboard comes in several textures—smooth, striated, corrugated, and

LIGHT AND AIRY, this wood screen is made of 1 by 2 strips which were hand cut; it hides parking area.

CRISSCROSSED THIN LATH forms a light, tall fence to mask a good portion of the solid brick wall.

PLYWOOD PANELS ARE FRAMED WITH grooved posts, black wrought iron grillwork. Note the old round caps.

perforated. Usually one side of an interior hardboard panel is smooth surfaced; the other is often screen textured. Only the tempered variety, which is smooth on both sides, should be used for exterior construction. No matter what the texture, hardboard can be painted, and it offers good resistance to weather. It is available in standard 4 foot widths, and in lengths of 7 to 16 feet.

Like most paneling materials, hardboard needs stringer support between the fence posts to prevent it from bowing. Expansion and contraction should be allowed for at the joints.

Asbestos Board Paneling

One of the most durable materials available for fencing is asbestos board, which is manufactured of asbestos and cement. It is not only extremely resistant to the normal effects of weather, but it is also fireproof, rot and rustproof, and rodent and termite repellent.

Asbestos board is a very heavy material to work with (a 4 by 8-foot, 1/4-inch-thick panel weighs 80 pounds, the 1/2-inch thickness twice as much) and requires heavy support posts.

Standard sizes are 4 feet wide by 4, 8, 10, and 12-foot lengths in 1/8, 3/16, 1/4, 3/8, and 1/2-inch thicknesses. The thicker panels are recommended for fencing and outdoor use. The panels are available in flat or corrugated configurations, and the natural color is stone gray. Though no painting or preservative treatment is required, asbestos board can be painted if you first apply a water base primer. For convenience, it is available in an al-

ready-primed version ready for final painting. Asbestos sheets are manufactured in almost every color imaginable.

The panels can be sawn, but a simpler method of cutting is to score them with an ice pick and snap them. Predrilling of nail holes is not required, and because the asbestos resists splitting, it can be nailed very near the edge.

The Prefabricated Fence

There is a growing trend towards factory prefabrication and pre-assembly of fencing. Not long ago, prefabricated fencing was limited to just a few standard designs, but now it can be ordered in almost every major type of wood fence. Most fences are available in either ready-to-assemble components, or complete pre-assembled panels.

One of the most popular prefabricated designs is the basket weave, which is offered in many variations by most fencing manufacturers. Another popular ready-to-erect style is the post and rail. These fences are available in a range of styles from components made of rough, round or split posts and rails to more sophisticated versions with square posts and smooth surfaced rails.

Probably the most familiar prefabricated fence (also the most convenient and versatile) is the rustic woven wood fence. This fence comes in a wide variety of materials—pickets, saplings, reed, and bamboo—and is available in both rolls and panels.

The woven wood fence is adaptable to almost any casual, informal, or rustic setting. It has the

SOLID WOOD PANELS are contrasted with darkly stained posts and rails to create a handsome entryway.

BAMBOO STRIPS soften appearance and create decorative interest in board fence; note bamboo gate panels.

surface texture of a closely spaced picket fence which complements growing plants and vines, and forms an effective barrier in the yard. It is also very durable, and weathers attractively.

This type of prefabricated fencing is available in several styles: peeled, machine finished, or complete with bark; round or half-round; wired together or strung on steel rods. The wood is usually cedar, the variety depending upon the local species. Manufacturers in the Midwest and Northwest produce the largest number of these fences, and prices increase in proportion to the distance from the factory. If you order direct from the manufacturer, you may get a discount that approximates the shipping costs.

Big lumber producers and various lumber associations will supply information on their lines of prefabricated fences. Other good sources of information are local fence contractors and lumber dealers.

The Bamboo Fence

Bamboo is a very old and common fencing material. More than 700 species of bamboo are known to exist—200 of them grow in the Western Hemisphere. Although suitable bamboo can be hand cut in many parts of the world, in the western United States bamboo husky enough for fencing must be obtained from lumberyards.

One of the most compatible of materials to use in a garden, bamboo is used most effectively in fences as a contrasting panel alternating with finished lumber. However, all-bamboo fences can be extremely attractive if placed in the right situation and garden.

Bamboo can be lashed together with any type of wire or heavy cord. (*Bamboo cannot be nailed, as it will split.*) The Japanese often use *shuro nawa*, a dark, fuzzy twine that contrasts attractively with the light color of bamboo. *Shuro nawa* can be approximated by dipping any heavy, fuzzy wrapping cord in creosote.

As shown in the drawing below, you lash vertical and horizontal members together with the cord. Use a plain square knot and let the ends extend an inch or so. Tie horizontal pieces to posts with several lashings.

Large timber bamboo or several smaller culms (as the poles are called) lashed together make strong fence posts, but if you sink untreated bamboo into the ground to serve as a post, it probably will rot out within two or three years. If treated with pentachlorophenol, it will last longer. The best approach is to use wood posts for support and keep the bamboo off the ground.

Note in the drawing that you cut the tops of vertical pieces of bamboo just above the joints. This prevents rain and dust from collecting inside. You can also cut the ends at an angle with the bottoms of the slants just above the joints. This leaves sharp ends to discourage climbers.

For a privacy screen, you can lash the culms close together instead of spacing them. Another Japanese custom is to erect two open-spaced fences 1 to 3 feet apart and plant a hedge between them.

READY TO ASSEMBLE fence panels are sold in variety of styles. Illustrated are rail, picket, basketweave.

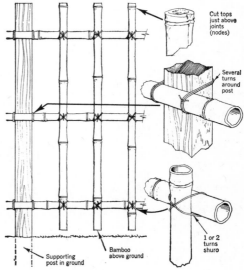

TYPICAL CONSTRUCTION of bamboo fence shows vertical, horizontal members lashed together with cord.

VARIATIONS OF THE BASIC WOOD FENCE

All of the wood fences discussed in this chapter have been constructed in the same basic manner. Either fences were simple post and rail, or the posts and rails formed the framework to which siding was attached. This type of wood fencing is the most common, but there are variations.

The Palisade Fence

This fence is built entirely with posts. Each post functions as a picket and is embedded in the ground. Because each post is self-supporting, there is no need for connecting rails (though slimmer pickets should be wired together to keep them in alignment). An advantage of this fence is that it can follow the contours of a curving, uneven boundary better than any other fence. Some of the most unusual and attractive results have been obtained by using bulky materials, such as railroad ties and sections of telephone poles.

The Stacked Fence

Railroad ties can be stacked horizontally to form a bulky, solid fence which is held together by vertical steel rods inserted through drilled holes. A stacked fence of this type usually supports itself by its own weight.

STURDY, CURVING palisade fence is made with overlapping boards nailed together, imbedded in concrete.

ROUNDING A CURVE is simple for railless palisade fence. Grapestakes are set in concrete, wired together.

RAILROAD TIES can be stacked horizontally to form a sturdy boundary fence or imbedded into the ground vertically to form an attractive low edging that offsets sparse but carefully placed shrubs.

GOOD NEIGHBOR FENCES

The term "good neighbor" is likely to crop up in any discussion of fences. Rather than describing a specific type of fence, the expression refers to any fence which is attractive on both sides. Some good neighbor fences (basket weave, board and board) appear identical on both sides; others present different faces. Pictured below are a few of more popular choices of good neighbor fences.

BOARD AND BOARD fence has alternating panels of same size; middle rails break up lumber expanse.

THIN BATTENS add interest to frame side of solid board fence, provide good support for plants.

REDWOOD SLATS are placed at angles in alternating horizontal and vertical panels; permit ample light.

VERTICAL POSTS in inside view of solid board fence attract the eye, complement tall trees beyond.

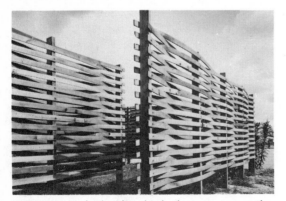

IDENTICAL on both sides, this basketweave screen has slats woven around 2 by 4's slightly spaced apart.

SLENDER POSTS add formal touch, frame horizontal grapestakes; appearance is same on both sides.

TWO VIEWS of tall screen show progressive privacy achieved by proper spacing of slats. Screen looks solid in angled view (left), lets in light, glimpses of neighboring foliage when viewed head on.

SOLID WOOD PANELS faced with vertical strips and topped with open frame form plant background.

SCREEN AND DECK form a garden pavilion which hides house trailer; open roof extends over trailer.

REED AND BATTENS form panels for Japanese-styled fence; posts are anchored to steel plates in concrete.

CLOSED BOARD and massive posts give solid protected look to entryway; post caps accent tiled roof.

STREETSIDE TRELLIS supports Virginia creeper, gives an open feeling while still providing privacy.

BATTENS AND BOARDS used on house at left are repeated in fence and landscape design to give unity.

TALL SLAT SCREEN forms support for growing vines, provides privacy and blocks view of house next door.

LIGHTWEIGHT SCREEN of 1 by 2 slats is set on top of brick wall to form interesting, airy entryway.

HONEYSUCKLE climbs easily, informally on this screen of 1 by 1 redwood slats. 1 by 4's form frame.

THIN STRIPS form screen, admit sunlight and breezes and provide privacy. Posts are made of 2 by 4's.

CONSTRUCTION DETAILS

Board Fence

Board fences are relatively simple to construct—they usually can be assembled quite rapidly once the posts are erected. Because they are generally heavy, and often subject to wind damage, a substantial foundation is required.

The choice of designs is up to the builder's imagination. Boards can be opened, separated like pickets, or overlapped to form a closed louver effect. They can be placed vertically or horizontally, and they may be alternated with other materials.

One-sided fences can be avoided by designing the frame side so it has strong interest in itself; by fitting the boards wholly within the frame so the fence appears the same from both sides; or by adding decoration and plantings.

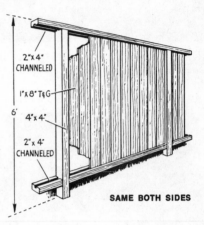

SAME BOTH SIDES

Picket Fence

Pickets can be found cut and ready to install at many lumberyards, but choice in top designs is limited. Those who decide to cut their own pickets should keep the design simple, and work with standard width lumber.

To construct a picket fence, first build the basic post-and-rail frame, then attach the pickets (these steps are described in detail on page 24).

The sketch below illustrates an easy way to keep picket bottoms aligned as you proceed.

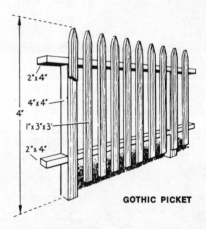

GOTHIC PICKET

If you need to protect the fence against digging animals, finish it with a baseboard buried a few inches into the soil (or nail chicken wire to the bottom and bury it a few inches in the soil).

Another good idea is to nail a molding strip on the outside of the fence, parallel to the top rail to protect the pickets from being worked loose or pulled off.

Louver Fence

Louver fences require more material than most of the other wood fences, and their construction is somewhat more complicated. There are two ways to build louver fences: drive nails through the top rail into the louver, and toenail the louver to the bottom rail; or construct the fence in sections on the ground, and lift the panels into place, nailing them to the posts. The second method is probably the easiest if you have a flat surface to work on.

Though the accepted angle for attaching louvers is 45 degrees, they can be set at almost any angle. For accurate spacing, use a template as shown in the drawing. Ideally, the boards should be kiln dried, and heavy enough to resist warping. A slanted or beveled top rail helps to protect the louvers from water. If privacy is important, be sure to choose the angle of the louvers carefully.

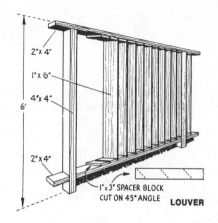

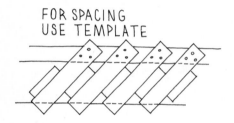

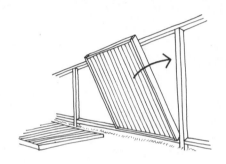

Basket Weave Fence

Basket weave fences are easy to build once construction techniques are mastered. Wooden slats for weaving between the posts should be no less than 1/2 nor more than 1-inch thick. A favored width for these strips is 6 inches, but they can be narrower or wider. It is a good idea to use standard lengths of lumber with 4 by 4-inch posts spaced accordingly. Nail the ends of the slats to alternating posts for a strong fence.

Spacers (vertical boards the slats are woven around between posts) can also be various sizes depending upon the finished look that is desired. The smaller the spacers, the closer the weave.

Rails at the top and bottom of the fence are optional, depending upon the design of the fence.

For a simple basket weave fence, nail all the strips to one side of the posts (leaving just enough space for clearance of a spacer), and then weave in the spacers from the top.

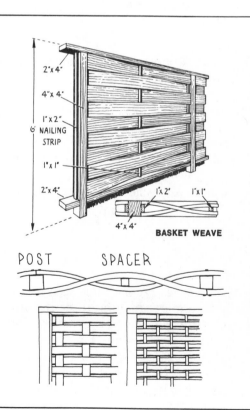

PATTERNED GLASS screens entryway and side yard, admits filtered sunlight.

Fences of Other Materials

Although wood is the most commonly used fencing material, there are other materials that can do the job as well and can also provide an interesting and unusual effect. Of these materials, glass, plastic, asbestos, aluminum, masonry, wrought iron, and wire are the most popular. Wire is so commonly used that it is discussed separately on page 62. The cost, availability, appearance, endurance, and difficulties of installation vary with each product.

Glass

Glass is the ideal material for shutting out the wind while maintaining a view. Along some sections of the coast where summer temperatures remain generally cool and where the view is part of the living scheme, glass screening is particularly effective. Transparent glass windscreens are also a good solution to updrafts or winds that may blow through the outdoor living area of a house located on an exposed hilltop.

A glass screen may also be particularly welcome alongside a swimming pool as a protection from the wind. In areas where summer heat is not a problem, glass screens can give a garden wind protection without a loss of sunshine. Where privacy and light are desired, obscure glass can be used. Glass and other solid panels, however, are not always the best solution to a wind problem (see pages 8-9).

The two main objections to the use of glass as a screening material are its expense and the fact that it is hard to work with.

Glass is a fragile construction material. It will bend slightly under steady pressure, but will not withstand wrenching or jerking. Therefore, a glass windscreen must be built solidly to resist not only buffeting by the wind, but also any shifting or settling of the soil.

In most cases, amateur handymen should not attempt to construct glass screens. Working with glass generally requires special talents—especially where cutting is involved.

Glass suitable for screens is available in several textured patterns, and a variety of colors and tints. It is also available in both tempered and untempered sheets. *Only approved safety glass is recommended for use in glass screens.*

Plastic Fencing Materials

When light transmission rather than visual clarity is an important function of the screen or fence, plastic is a practical material to use. Plastic is also one of the most versatile of fencing materials where special effects are desired, as it can be produced in almost every color and degree of translucence.

Plastic screening. One of the earliest uses of plastic in fencing consisted of common window screening material sealed in a plastic sandwich. This screening is now available in many combinations. It is found made of woven plastic fibers, with or without the plastic sandwich, in various sizes of mesh, and in many different colors. Depending upon the closeness of the mesh and the color density, this material also has a variable range of light transmission.

Plastic screening can be used for many different situations. It can diffuse sunlight to a soft radiance that reflects a feeling of coolness in the garden and, used as a screen to silhouette plants, it can give the appearance of a subtly executed Japanese print. Plastic screening can also perform more functional services, such as screening off pools, service areas, or outside traffic, or it can simply be used to keep insects out.

One of the best functions of plastic screening is as a climate modifier. The screening can cut wind velocity and reduce light transmission. Plants that windburn in an open garden may thrive behind a screened panel, and other plants may welcome the reduced light intensity.

The quality that endears plastic screening to the homeowner is that it is cheaper to buy and install than rigid plastic or glass. However, it often proves to be more expensive because of repairs and replacement.

Plastic screening should be installed with battens or molding strips for easy removal in case of damage.

Plastic panels. Fiberglass and other types of plastic panels are available in flat sheets, corrugated and ribbed panels, and in just about every color and pattern imaginable. Textures, patterns, and original designs may even be incorporated into the plastic. One such version comes in flat panels with bright awning stripes and can be obtained with grooved wooden posts for quick and simple assembly.

Plastic panels are practically impervious to weather as far as strength and endurance is concerned, but some colors have a tendency to dull and fade after long exposure to sunlight. Surface erosion and scratching may impair the light transmission. Concentrated garden sprays and other chemicals may also be injurious. For plastic that has been abused there are commercial products that help to restore the finish.

Installation of plastic panels is usually not too difficult, because they are lightweight and can be

TRANSLUCENT GLASS screen brings privacy to enclosed garden. Sun silhouettes plants beyond glass wall.

PIVOTING FIBERGLASS PANELS can be adjusted to any angle for privacy, sun, and wind control.

TRANSLUCENT GLASS SCREEN blocks desert wind and provides privacy for open sections of walled garden.

FIBERGLASS PANELS set in dark wood frame at far corner of garden protect outdoor dining area.

SECURITY, the prime consideration for this garden, was achieved by building this ornamental aluminum fence.

ORNAMENTAL IRON attached to concrete wall forms background for flowering plants; gate repeats design.

ADOBE BRICK is combined with open grillwork to give secure, yet warm feeling to this front yard fence.

CONCRETE AND BRICK structure has fleur-de-lis pattern; has solid look outside, light and airy feeling inside.

easily cut and nailed in place. To prevent crazing along the saw cut, use a fine-toothed hand saw, or a power tool with an abrasive disc. It is wise to pre-drill all nail holes to avoid shock marks and use aluminum nails and neoprene washers for fastening.

Masonry Grilles—Heavy and Ornamental

The grille is an ancient device developed in the Mediterranean and the warm areas of the Orient to control the heat and glare of bright sun, and to achieve privacy and protection from the outside while still permitting those inside to see out. Today, for the same reasons, masonry grillwork is very popular in Southern California and the Southwest desert.

Masonry grilles are most commonly built of concrete block, but a grillwork screen can also be constructed from flue and drain tile sections, and bricks stacked in varying positions and patterns.

Concrete blocks are available at most lumber and masonry outlets. Although quite heavy, these blocks are easy to use, and their large size permits rapid construction of a good-sized screen.

One problem in adapting a masonry grille to a home or garden situation is toning down its extreme ornamental design. Careful placement of plants in front of grillwork is usually quite successful in relieving this often overwhelming pattern.

For further information on masonry installations, see the *Sunset* book, *How to Build Walks, Walls, & Patio Floors.*

Ornamental Metal Fencing

Ornamental iron fences—like Victorian houses and old-fashioned picket fences—are holdovers

---

GLASS—BEAUTIFUL AND HAZARDOUS

ORDINARY GLASS shatters into sharp, dagger-like pieces when struck, can produce serious cuts.

TEMPERED GLASS breaks into sizable round chunks; is available in plate or sheet, clear or patterned.

The U. S. Public Health Service estimates that more than 100,000 Americans are injured, many of them fatally, each year by walking or falling through glass doors and panels. More than a third of the victims are children.

Most of these accidents can be prevented with the use of approved safety glass or plastic in hazardous areas.

If you live in a community that has adopted adequate glass regulations—or if FHA financing is involved—the new house you buy, build, or remodel is required to have safety glass or approved rigid plastic in all hazardous areas. The materials that are permitted include fully tempered glass, wired glass, laminated glass, and rigid plastic. These materials will not break readily—and if they do, the chances of bad cuts are minimal.

If you have existing installations of untempered glass, you can still take steps to make sure that no one mistakes a panel of glass for an opening. (Even if you have safety glass, it is a good idea to take precautionary measures.) One way to point out that your glass door or glass screen is no passageway is to place furniture or plants in such a way that they control traffic. Another way is to place highly visible decals on the glass panels, or hang decorative mobiles or plants in front of them. Along a glass-screened entryway you might even install a handsome wood rail.

IRON PICKETS and massive concrete posts are over-grown with vines, give suburban road old-world look.

STUCCO was applied to fence frame with same procedure as for house exterior; posts accent house trim.

BRICK BAFFLE SCREEN gives privacy to window. Bricks rest on concrete, are reinforced with steel rods.

HOLLOW CONCRETE BLOCKS form self-supporting screen. Reinforcing rods are set in blocks horizontally.

BRICK WALL-FENCE, iron gate, green shrubs, give this desert-edge garden a secure, but cool and open look. Bricks repeat material of house; vines grow through open space in wall.

DIAMOND-SHAPED CONCRETE BLOCKS placed on end form this decorative but completely private screen.

SLUMP BLOCK, mortared together vertically adapts easily and gracefully to curve of driveway.

PRE-CAST CONCRETE BLOCKS form distinctive pattern for screen which serves as background for desert plants.

ALUMINUM can be utilized in many forms. Expanded aluminum panel (left) can be used in place of wire. Aluminum screen (right) is mounted on a track, provides movable shade for side of house.

from an earlier era. There are still many ornamental iron fences throughout the West—many in a state of deterioration, others lovingly restored by new owners.

Many urban architects have effectively paired updated ornamental fencing of aluminum, bronze, and steel with sleek, modern townhouses and city homes. Particularly attractive is the contrast between a modern white stucco structure and black, metal picket fencing.

Manufacturers of ornamental metal fencing offer a wide variety of railing and finial designs. These fences can be made to almost any specifications, if cost is not a consideration.

Aluminum Panel Fencing

A relatively recent development in prefabricated fencing is the aluminum panel system. The choices of designs in aluminum fencing vary from an adaptation of the traditional Gothic picket, to versions of familiar wood designs such as board, board on board, basket weave, post and rail, louvers, and solid panels. Many of the panels can be installed with either aluminum posts or wood posts. Because many persons consider the natural look of aluminum out of place in a residential garden, manufacturers offer the fencing in a wide variety of baked enamel colors and finishes. Depending upon the style, the fencing is available in different heights. Rail and picket types are usually 3 to 4 feet high and the board and basket weave styles can be ordered in high fence sizes.

Aluminum fencing offers many of the same advantages as other metals—permanence, strength, and low maintenance and repair. Careful placement of plants is important along an aluminum fence as it is with most fences made of nonwood materials, which are not indigenous to a garden setting.

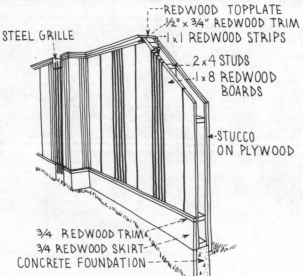

DUAL PERSONALITY fence was solution for this homeowner. Exterior of modern townhouse called for sleek, stucco fence (right) and interior Japanese garden required softer look of wood.

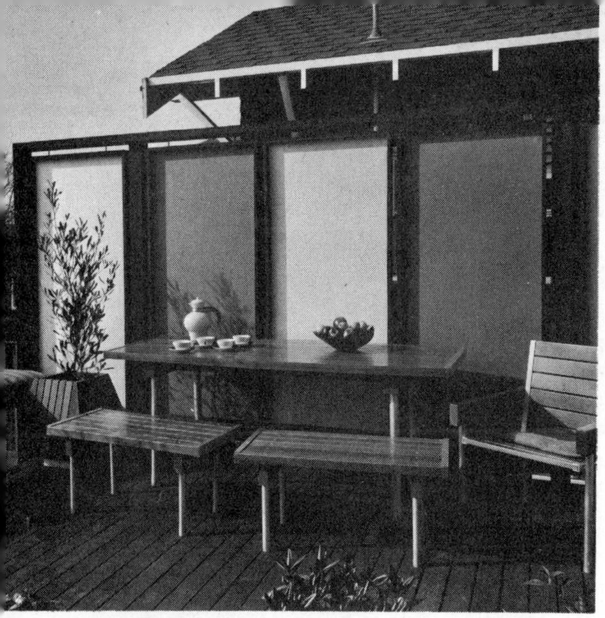

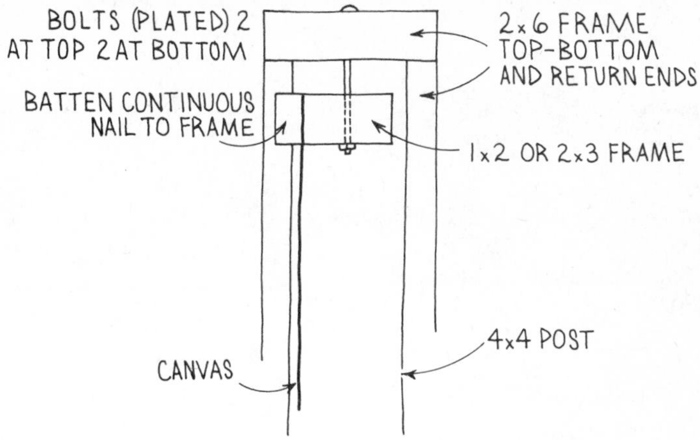
BOLTS (PLATED) 2
AT TOP 2 AT BOTTOM
BATTEN CONTINUOUS
NAIL TO FRAME
2x6 FRAME
TOP-BOTTOM
AND RETURN ENDS
1x2 OR 2x3 FRAME
4x4 POST
CANVAS

CANVAS can be used for bright, colorful screening. Sketch shows simple construction details.

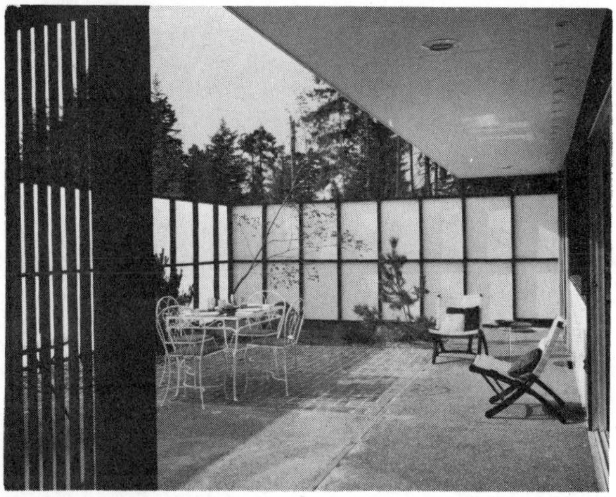

WHITE FIBERGLASS PANELS, contrasting handsomely with dark wood frames, enclose two sides of patio.

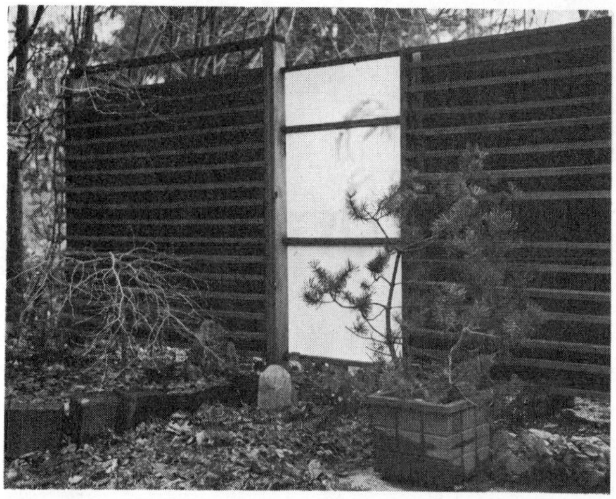

WINDOW of white plastic adds a bright note to fence, catches winter sun and silhouettes tree behind it.

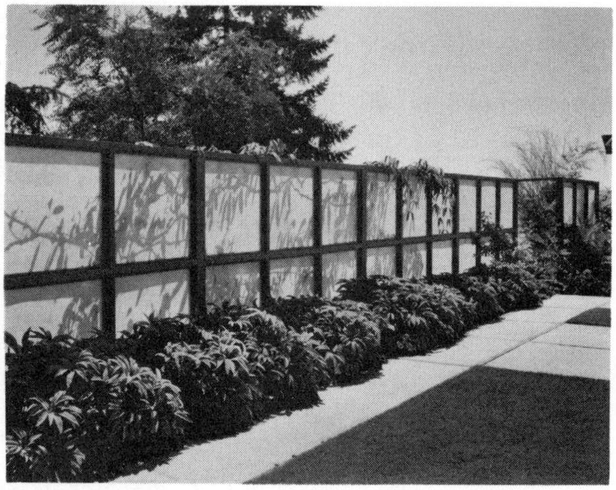

SHADOW PATTERN of Clematis armandii *plays on a plastic screen which blocks view of neighbors.*

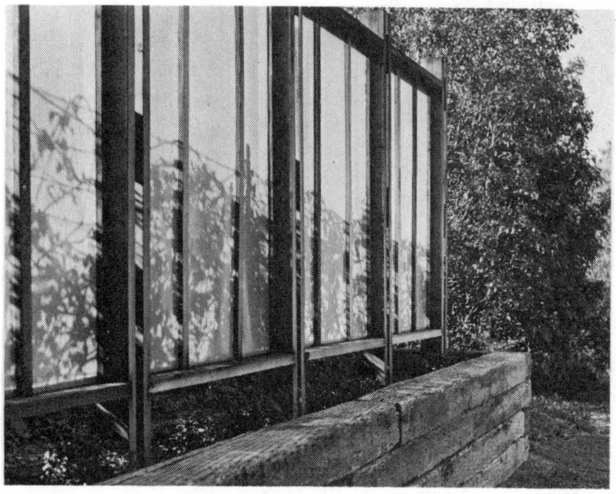

LIGHTWEIGHT PLASTIC in wood frame tops raised bed built of railroad ties. Screen admits ample light.

WIRE combined with wood, plantings, forms handsome boundary fence.

Wire For Security and Practicality

Where security is the primary need—whether to discourage intruders and vandals or to confine children, pets, and domestic animals—wire is the superior choice of all fence materials.

Most of the wire materials long associated with country fencing have made a comfortable transition to the city—with the exception of barbed and electric wire which are prohibited by most urban building codes.

WIRE IN THE CITY

Although wire has played a lengthy role as the ugly duckling of fence materials for residential communities, imaginative fence builders are finding more and more ways of combining it with other materials to produce a fence that is reasonably attractive. There is also an increasing trend toward using it as a natural support for plantings and vines and as a quick and economical solution to fencing within a yard, such as around a vegetable garden, a dog run, a play yard, or a swimming pool. The homeowner can choose between two basic types of wire fence.

Wire and Wood Fences

The most commonly used combination in this type of fencing is wire mesh attached to wooden posts. When rails are added, the fence becomes even more interesting. Strands of wire may be combined with a post-and-board fence or the framing may be designed to harmonize with the geometric pattern of the wire mesh.

The pattern and weight of the wire you select depends upon the design and degree of security you need. Posts used with wood-and-mesh fences can either be squared lumber obtainable from a lumber dealer, or round, peeled logs made from timber cut on the site. If squared posts are used, the choice of wood is the same as for any other type of fence, but if round posts are used, the selection is wide open. Many varieties of wood that never turn up in the lumberyard make excellent fence posts if they are properly treated with preservatives. Recommended woods are: redwood, cedar, cypress, oak, catalpas, and madrone.

All-metal Wire Fences

These fences are manufactured as complete units. The buyer is provided with posts, rails, mesh, gates, hinges, and all other fittings.

A popular choice for keeping children and pets confined, the all-metal fence comes in various patterns which are quite difficult to climb. Aesthetically, metal fencing is often not pleasing to look at, but with continued new developments in the field, it is becoming more attractive.

There are several types of all-metal wire fences but the two styles that have become the most familiar in urban use are the woven metal picket and the chain link (see drawings).

The metal picket fence. Readily available in both single and double picket styles in 36, 42, and 48-inch rolls or strips, the single picket is also sold for quick fencing of flower beds or borders in 16 and 22-inch heights. No posts are required—you simply push the wire into the ground.

Wire picket fencing is normally made of galvanized steel but it is also available in aluminum and plastic coated styles.

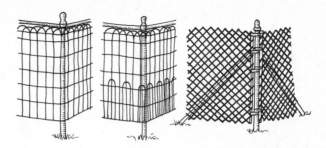

ALL STEEL chain link and woven pickets in single, double styles, come as complete, ready to erect units.

The chain link fence. The most familiar chain link fence is made of galvanized steel which has been processed in two ways. One type is galvanized after the mesh has been woven and a second type is dipped prior to weaving. Those dipped after weaving are more rustproof.

Chain link comes in 36, 42, and 48-inch heights as well as heights from 5 to 9 feet (and sometimes higher). Eleven-gauge chain link is satisfactory for home use but it is available in thicker gauges (such as 9 and 6-gauge) for heavier duty. For home fencing, the usual thickness of wire is 11 to 14½-gauge.

Besides galvanized steel, the chain link fence comes in aluminum-coated steel, aluminum alloy, and, in one of the newest innovations—plastic-coated steel. The plastic coating is permanently bonded to the chain link. These varieties are available in a wide range of colors—though availability and selection varies in different parts of the

WELDED WIRE mesh fence is designed to keep dogs out. Wire look is softened by plantings of marguerite.

POSTS of woven wire fence are anchored in concrete. Pointed finials, medallions, add decorative touch.

PLASTIC, WOOD STRIPS in a variety of colors and finishes can be inserted into chain link to dress it up.

REDWOOD PICKETS are woven into steel chain link to produce fence more fitted to a residential setting.

country. The most common color is a forest green, which blends in nicely with foliage. Other colors on the market are blue, white, pink, sandalwood, yellow, redwood, black, and combinations of blue and white, green and white, and black and white.

The insertion of wood, plastic, or metal strips in various colors into the chain link fence is another variation in the continuing effort to make this type of fencing more attractive. These woven strips are normally inserted vertically, but variations call for horizontal, diagonal, or criss-cross insertions. The most familiar of the interwoven chain link fences is the one that utilizes redwood pickets vertically. Addition of the strips provides maximum security and privacy and also enhances the appearance of the fence.

Metal posts for chain link fences are available in a variety of styles and shapes. Many fences use round pipe for corners, line posts, and connecting rails. Line posts may also be channeled into U or H shapes. Square posts and rails are also appearing with greater frequency, and many builders feel they contribute a crisper, more tailored look to chain link. Some galvanized chain link posts are coated with a clear plastic for better resistance to weather. (Construction pointers for stretching and installing wire fences are given on pages 66-67.)

WIRE IN THE COUNTRY—BY THE ACRE

In the country a fence still has the significance it had in grandfather's day: it excludes unwanted livestock and other creatures, it holds in domestic animals, and it preserves local harmony. The city dweller's considerations of privacy, space division, and outdoor living don't mean much in a rural setting where there is a half-mile between neighbors.

Cost alone dictates that country fencing be more open and less decorative than city fencing. Barbed wire and woven wire are the standard, multipurpose materials in rural areas, but there are also situations that call for specialized materials such as chain link, electric fencing, post and rail, and board fences.

The Barbed Wire Fence

Barbed wire is the more economical of the two multipurpose fences. It's sold by the rod, which is 16½ feet (if an acre is square, it measures 12½

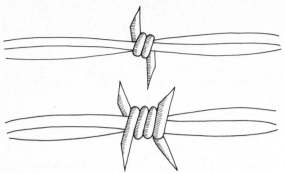

BARBED WIRE comes in wide variety of barb styles and spacing, but two and four point are most popular.

rods on each side). Price for barbed wire depends on the gauge of wire, the number of barbs (two or four points), and barb spacing (usually four or five inches apart). Barbed wire is also available in several styles with 3 and 6-inch barb spacing. Fourteen-gauge barbed wire is inexpensive, and lightweight; the more costly, heavy-duty type is 12½ gauge. Both types are heavily galvanized. Some styles are available in more expensive high-tensile-strength steel.

Barbed wire can injure children and tear clothing, so it isn't satisfactory—and is usually against the law—near houses. It's best used to hold livestock in large, open-country fields.

The Woven Wire Fence

The National Bureau of Standards of the U. S. Department of Commerce has categorized woven

STEEL CHAIN LINK is best choice for desired security. This movable fence guards, closes off pool area.

wire to be within eight standard sizes (see chart).

The 47-inch size with 10 line wires is probably the best choice for fencing several acres. It is high and strong enough to stop all domestic animals. Some poultry fences are made in the same pattern, but generally of lighter wire (11 to 15½ gauge); are higher (36 to 72 inches); and have more line wires (19, 20, 21, 23, and 26). Although it is made for poultry, it can be used successfully as temporary livestock fencing.

Good grades of woven wire have tension curves or crimps in the line wires between each stay. These crimps allow for contraction and expansion when the temperature changes. One type of woven wire has squares of the same size all the way down. It comes in 3, 4, and 6-foot heights.

The Poultry Netting Fence

This fence material is lightweight wire (20 gauge) formed into square or hexagonal mesh. Even under ideal support and tension, it is only strong enough to pen up poultry, though it discourages small animals from entering the hen yard. The material

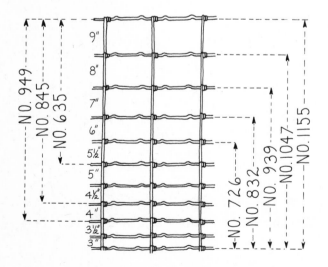

WOVEN WIRE is standardized into eight styles shown here. Different spacings serve variety of purposes.

serves well for a short time around small yards, but woven wire poultry fencing offers better service.

You can buy hexagonal poultry netting in one-inch and two-inch mesh (the smaller type is recommended for chicks) and in heights ranging from 12 to 72 inches. It is available either galvanized before or after weaving. The latter is more rustproof and costs more.

The Steel Chain Link Fence

For a strong, practically indestructible fence that requires little upkeep and cannot be climbed, nothing beats a steel chain link fence. Compared with other fencing, however, it is expensive—especially in the country where fencing requirements are measured by the acre. The high initial cost, however, can be balanced by the long life of the fence. It should last a lifetime, while other types take replacement about every 20 years. Steel or aluminum chain link fences are particularly good for enclosing house yards, play areas, pump houses, and water supplies.

The Electric Fence

The value of an electric fence has always been a matter of controversy. In its favor: it requires only one strand of wire and can be shifted easily or installed temporarily to protect crops from stock invasion, or to control stock grazing. In its disfavor: under some circumstances, it presents a serious shock hazard, particularly to children; it requires constant maintenance (weeds can ground it out); loose connections develop that reduce its efficiency; it can cause radio interference; stock must be educated to respect it, otherwise they may wander right through it; and if current fails, part or all of an entire fence loses its value.

Most states have laws governing these fences, so before you install one, first check your local building codes, then talk to manufacturers, your county agent, and the local power or public utilities representative.

HOW TO CONSTRUCT WIRE FENCES

Construction of most wire fences is within the capacity of a skilled handyman who can follow directions carefully, but it is a project that is best completed by two persons. As a rule, installation of a long stretch of chain link fence is best entrusted to a contractor who specializes in this type of construction.

The main difficulty the amateur will encounter is stretching the fence wire taut. This requires special tools and presents some hazard to an inexperienced builder. A long length of fencing may require a pull of several hundred pounds to get it to proper tension.

If you decide to attempt the job yourself, send 15 cents to the U. S. Government Printing Office, Division of Public Documents, Washington, D. C. 20402, and ask for the U. S. Department of Agriculture Farmer's Bulletin 2173, *Farm Fences,* which gives detailed building instructions.

Here are the principal steps in building wire fences.

Setting the Posts

The most common spacing for wire fence posts is 10 feet. If you are using wood posts, installation is basically the same as for an all-wood fence (see page 19) with one exception: the original stretching of the wire and the subsequent additional shrinkage in cold weather puts a tremendous amount of pressure on the posts. You will therefore need stronger corner, gate, and end post installations—bigger posts, deeper set and with bracing—than called for with the all-wood fence.

Although the setting of steel posts is often done by driving them in place (using either a sleeve-type driver made for this purpose or a sledge), setting the end, corner, and gate posts in concrete will result in a stronger installation. The size and depth of the hole required will vary, depending on the height of the fence and whether the soil is loose or firm. The U. S. Department of Agriculture recommends that you set steel corner and end posts $3\frac{1}{2}$ to 4 feet in the ground with the hole for the concrete base 18 inches square at the top and 20 inches square at the bottom. Most contractors consider a 3-foot hole with a 12 inch diameter to be adequate for the normal 6-foot residential wire installation. It is usually a good idea to dig the hole wider at the bottom.

Bracing and anchoring end and corner posts. There are various ways of providing extra strength for wire fence posts. Several types of easy-to-install steel post anchors are on the market. Wood posts can be given more stability with the simple addition of wooden cleats to the below-ground portion. Other solutions are above-ground corner braces, diagonal tie wires or braces, or horizontal rails. Combinations of these supports are often used for added strength.

Stretching the Wire

Wire fencing should be stretched before it is permanently fastened to the posts. This can be a difficult and trying job. For a short stretch of fence, brute strength may do an adequate job, but for longer fences, use a block and tackle or a stretcher which is manufactured specifically for this job. Never use an automobile or truck to stretch wire. This is dangerous—because an overstretched wire can snap and whiplash. Also, you are more apt to overstretch a fence when using motive power.

First, unroll about 25 feet of wire along the ground with one end next to a corner post. In order to fasten the wire to the first post, you will have to trim two or three stay wires (vertical) from the end so that each line wire (horizontal) can be wrapped around the post and then back around itself four or five turns. Stand the wire up with the last stay wire at the end of the post and begin fastening the wires, starting with the center wire and working up and down.

Continue unrolling until you reach the end of the roll or a point where the mesh is to be cut (as at an end or a corner post). Fasten a heavy pipe, bar, or strong piece of wood to the free end of the wire, and attach the pulling device to it. Anchor

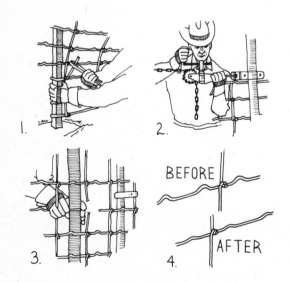

WIRE STRETCHING is illustrated here: attach one end to post, stretch wire to next post and fasten in place.

the other end to a dummy post, a tree, or an automobile, but not to an unbraced fence post. The best method is to use a dummy post with a heavy brace between it and the end or corner post.

When the slack is pulled out of the wire, and before releasing the pull, attach the mesh to the posts. Amateur fence builders often stretch wire too loosely, but it should not be pulled so tight that it will not be able to contract in cold weather.

Wire is stretched properly when the tension curves are about $2/3$ to $1/2$ the original depth and the wire is springy to the touch.

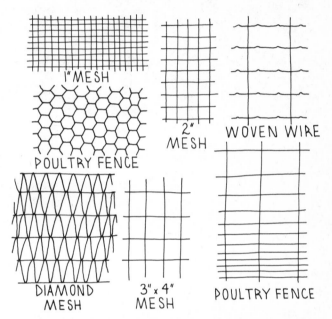

WIRE FENCING is available in wide variety of styles and sizes. Shown here are some of the most familiar.

On long fences, two rolls of wire can be stretched at the same time by attaching them to posts at the opposite ends of the line. Usually, wire mesh should be cut so the end just overlaps a post, but if it is necessary to end a stretch between posts, it can be spliced to the next roll (a job requiring skill). Wire should not be pulled around a corner. On curved fences, it must be brought around in a series of short, straight lengths. (For detailed information on bringing wire around a curve under tension, refer to the *Farm Fences* booklet mentioned on page 66. Another good source of information is the booklet *Contour Fencing* published by the Ohio Agriculture Research and Development Center, Wooster, Ohio 44691.) If the fence runs up and down hills, wire should be stretched from the points where grade changes.

POOL FENCE of reed and wood is practical, handsome.

Special Situation Fencing

There are many situations that call for special types of fencing. You may live in a wooded area which is a sanctuary for wild animals. To protect your vegetable garden or flower bed, a fence not only has to be sturdy but must provide an impregnable barrier against all sizes, shapes, and varying approaches of animals. Another situation may call for a fence that provides a great deal of shade. Still another requires a screen to blot out an eyesore on a sloping hillside without interfering with the view beyond. A fence can be designed to meet any one of a hundred different situations.

Pool Enclosures

Most communities now have ordinances that require homeowners with swimming pools to provide safeguards for protecting small children and nonswimmers. Homeowners usually translate this requirement into some sort of fence.

Any pool security fence should be made without horizontal toe-holds. A 4-inch mesh, for instance, provides just about the right toe space for a small child. Metal mesh should not be over 2 inches wide horizontally, and there should be no horizontal fence stringers or supports that could be climbed like a ladder. Louver and basket weave fences should be avoided. You should also be able to see through the pool fence from the house and patio.

If your yard is completely enclosed by a boundary fence, you may decide you have adequate pool protection. However, there are some powerful arguments for fencing the immediate pool area:

A boundary fence will screen out the neighborhood children, but it won't protect the toddlers in your own family. When you fence near the pool you keep most of the leaves and dirt from blowing into the water, thus reducing pool maintenance. A poolside fence provides more specific climate control since you can orient fence panels to block out chilling winds and create sun pockets that make swimming more enjoyable. It is probably best to arrange your fence to admit the afternoon sun, because most people swim more at that time of day.

Finally, by fencing the pool you separate and define the area devoted to swimmers. It is often possible to control the dressing room and lavatory traffic with fence panels, screening it away from the living room. A solid fence can provide the back wall for a dressing room or a pool cabana, and a single panel or a short free-standing fence can hide unsightly filtration and heating equipment.

Design elements of pool fences. Though security is the primary objective of pool fencing, don't overlook the design elements. There's no need to turn your pool area into a prison compound. Use plantings and decorative effects to help the fence blend into the landscape. Chain link fences, for example, which provide maximum security, are easy to mask with vines.

Movable pool fences. A good solution to the fenced-in feeling that comes with erection of a pool fence is a fence that can be moved or completely removed when the pool is in use. Fences can be mounted on tracks and wheels, or sections can be designed so that they pivot like big louvers,

permitting free access when they are open. Or the fence can be built of panels which can be lifted off their posts and set aside.

Horizontal Screens

Most people are so accustomed to seeing fences and screens in their normal, vertical position, that they tend to overlook the fact that fences can be placed horizontally for a special situation.

There are two places where horizontal screens are needed. One of these is the hillside lot. Most people who build on steep hillside lots do so because of the scenic views such property normally provides. However, the view is often spoiled by a disconcerting shorter view of a busy street or a neighbor's yard or house. The solution to the problem is often a simple matter of building a horizontal screen which extends the apparent ground level, screening out the undesired views.

Another place where horizontal screens are necessary is over a garden which is adjacent to a tall, neighboring house.

To function as a horizontal screen in the true sense of the word, it should be open—just a framework to support shrubs and vines. If you use solid materials, the screen becomes a deck or roof.

RETRACTABLE FENCES are effective barriers for pools when locked in place, can also be rolled out of the way when not needed. Most urban areas require pool fencing to protect small children.

WOVEN, pre-fabricated fence of half-round pine saplings makes an attractive pool fence. The same panels are used to form changing rooms. For complete privacy, plywood was set in panel centers.

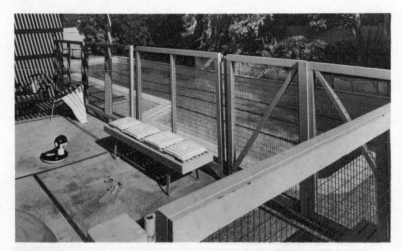

REMOVABLE, see-through panels of wire fencing keep children out of pool area when adults are not present. Panels lift out of supports on pipe posts; posts also lift out of sleeves in concrete.

HORIZONTAL SCREENS take many forms. Ground level screen at left has effect of extending deck, blocks view of street. Horizontal overhead screen at right blocks neighbor's bird's-eye view.

POOL MACHINERY peeks through slat screen in this straight on view. Backlighting at night dramatizes it.

GATE SECTIONS of steel chain link fence close off swimming area completely when pool is unsupervised.

POOL FENCE is also boundary fence. When pool is not near property line, another fence may be required.

SUNBATHING AREA utilizes spaced slats for privacy, wire mesh elsewhere preserves view of nearby hillsides.

TIED REED FENCE blends in nicely with garden foliage, is attractive by itself; here it hides pool equipment.

Movable Fences and Screens

Fences and screens which can be moved, rolled on tracks, or pivoted provide a whole new dimension in fencing possibilities.

One of the most obvious places for movable fences is around swimming pools, as discussed on page 68. But they can also be designed to perform many other functions. Several areas can be protected from the sun at different times of the day by simply moving a screen to shade the areas of intense heat. Or, when a movable screen is removed, it can open up a cozy garden area to accommodate a large group of people.

Utility Area Fencing

Fences can be used in several ways around the house to screen off and store unsightly tools and other paraphernalia, enclose a garden work center, or simply hide a trash or compost pile.

Garden work centers. All of the implements, pots, and materials which are needed by gardeners can be very unattractive if they are left out in open view. A good way to conceal this clutter is to place a screen between the garden and work areas using the back side of the screen for storage shelves. Another solution might be to build a roomy garden storage shed right into your fence. (Check with your city planning office about setback restrictions before building this type of structure.)

Trash enclosures. A familiar and unattractive sight in many communities is the weekly curbside storage of garbage and trash awaiting pickup. Another way to handle the problem would be to store the garbage cans in enclosures inside the streetside fence with access doors on the outside for trash collectors. (Again, check with your city building department about code restrictions for this type construction.)

MOVABLE FENCES take many forms. Wheel-mounted panel (top right) rolls easily along concrete strip. Panel (top left) can be lifted off, set aside. Lower photos show ways of controlling movable louvers.

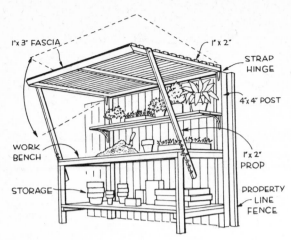

ATTACHED TO FENCE, this workbench has lath top which hinges down to protect plants. Storage is below.

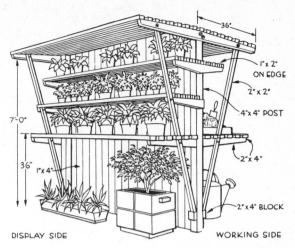

FREE-STANDING WORK CENTER is also a decorative screen and display area. Display side faces living areas.

DOUBLE-DECK STAND is made of 2 by 4's with 4 by 4 legs, provides ample plant display space against fence.

GARDEN WORK CENTER behind screen is simple and practical with plenty of space for pots, garden tools.

TRASH ENCLOSURE is provided by gate with two latch posts so it can be closed in two positions. Trash containers are normally inside, as shown at right, outside on trash collection mornings.

Storage fences. Garden equipment and trash containers are only two of the homeowner's storage problems. The accessories of outdoor living—sports equipment, children's toys, barbecue equipment, outdoor furniture—all create storage problems. A familiar solution is just to stack everything in the garage. A more convenient and attractive way to organize the storage of all this miscellaneous gear is to design a screen with built-in storage sections. Access can be provided from either or both sides.

Utility Fencing

If you need a temporary or economical fence, you may want to use the utility fence—a variety of the picket fence that is manufactured in roll form.

Utility fencing consists of dressed and painted pickets that are held in alignment by strands of galvanized wire, twisted between each picket. They are obtainable in natural finish, white, green, or red, with squared or pointed tops. They are sold in heights from 1½ to 6 feet, and in 50 or 110-foot rolls. Because of the long lengths of these rolls, utility fencing has to be cut more often than spliced. If splicing is necessary, a couple of lengths of strong wire twisted around adjacent end pickets will do the job quite satisfactorily.

Most utility fencing is made of wood that is not decay resistant and should therefore be kept from touching the ground. A baseboard will keep the pickets free of the ground and at the same time strengthen the fence.

Here are the steps for installing utility fencing:

1. Set posts and top and bottom rails, as described on pages 19-23. The lower rail is often omitted.

2. Unroll the fence on the ground alongside the posts.

3. Stand the fence against the posts and staple or nail it in place on one end post.

4. Stretch the fence taut and fasten it to the next post, using a board as a lever to tighten it. Insert the board through the fence next to the post and, using the post as a fulcrum, pull the fence tight and straight.

5. When the fence has been attached to the last post, staple or nail the top wire to the top rail.

Shade Fencing

Another type of utility fencing (also used as a screen) is the shade fence. Its construction is similar to utility fencing with 2-inch lath woven between galvanized wire. The shade fence comes

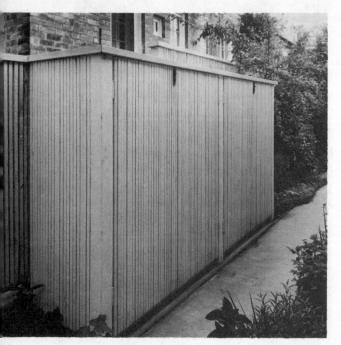

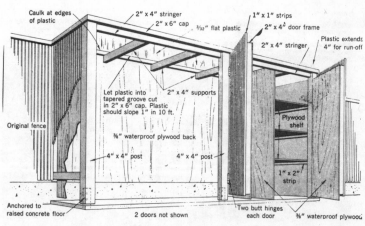

JOG IN FENCE forms a roomy garden shed. Each storage area has double doors and a translucent plastic top that lets in light. 1 by 1 cedar strips face both the fence and the shed.

in 1½ to 6-foot-wide rolls. Available in a variety of spacings between the laths to provide more or less shade, it can be used to shade plants, people, or animals, in temporary or permanent installations.

Suspension Fences

If you are using barbed wire to fence long distances, twisted wire stays can be a good substitute for intermediate line posts. This is a relatively new method, where the wire stays permit spacing of posts as far as 100 feet apart. The stays do not touch the ground and are placed where a line post would normally be set. Two different types of stays can be used to keep the barbed wire strands straight and in place. One is a single piece of wire which is doubled and then twisted. This permits it to be threaded down over the wires. The other type comes in two pieces—a coiled piece and a straight rod that holds it in place.

Fencing For Livestock

When building a fence, a rancher will consider the safety factors of the materials and styles he selects. Barbed wire has certain obvious disadvantages. Smooth wire, too, has certain dangers—a shod horse can catch a wire between shoe and hoof and cause serious injuries. If wire is used for enclosing horses, it should be closely woven. Chain-link is usually preferred by ranchers because of its strength and durability—but the cost per foot is quite high.

One new type of corral fencing is the post and rail variety, but it is constructed of round metal pipes. This fence is good for uneven land because the fittings swivel to follow the contour of the ground. The pipes can also be bent to follow a curving boundary line. Where a closed fence is desired, this type of fence can be adapted to chain link fabric.

Despite newer and more efficient uses of metal in fencing, wood fences seem to remain the favorite of ranchers.

The most common of the wood fences used for horses is the post and rail. Typical construction of this fence has rails or boards parallel to the ground and nailed to the inside of the posts to remove the danger of a horse hitting his shoulder as he gallops by. A flat board top from post to post will prolong the life of the fence by protecting it from sun and rain; it will also function as a brace. Slanted top boards shed the rain better, and discourage any "fence-walkers" in the neighborhood.

POST AND RAIL fence is suitable to country setting, good for containing livestock because of sturdiness.

STEEL POST AND RAIL is made from galvanized pipe, is adaptable to rolling terrain, and to curves.

Man Against the Rabbit

The continuing feud between rabbits and gardeners is well known. Rabbits eat garden plants on the fringes of suburbs, in the foothills, in summer cabin country—wherever the residential neighborhood fades into orchard, vineyard, chaparral, woods, or desert. They prefer vegetables, juicy young shoots, and any succulent growth—but they also nibble

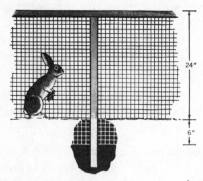

RABBIT-PROOF FENCE has portion of the wire buried. Rabbits can't hop over, squeeze through, or dig under.

APRON FENCES

There is an alternative to burying part of your fence underground to discourage burrowing animals. You can fold the bottom foot of the wire outward to form an apron and stake it down. A simpler and neater method is to purchase wire netting which is designed with an apron already attached and which will lay flatly in place when you unroll the fence. Several weeks of normal undergrowth should conceal and anchor the apron in place.

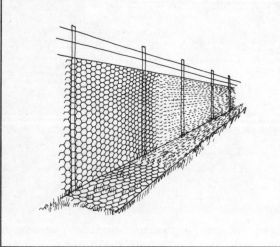

---

grass, summer flowers, all sorts of shrubs, and the bark and tender shoots of shade and fruit trees.

The only way to keep rabbits from eating your plants or vegetables is to build a wire mesh fence. The fence should be at least two feet high, and it should continue about six inches underground. Poultry wire is a good material to use, but whatever type of wire you choose, the mesh should not be wider than 1½ inches. The gates should fit tight and also have a 6-inch-deep underground barrier.

If it is impractical to use this type of fencing for the entire garden, you can still protect prized plants with poultry wire cylinders. Build them of 18 to 24-inch-wide wire mesh and brace them with stakes so that the rabbits can't push the wire inward to get within gnawing range. Cylinders are required for trees and shrubs only until they are too tall and strong for rabbits to do much damage.

Fences to Keep the Deer Out

The only sure way to keep deer out of a garden is to encircle it completely with an 8-foot fence of at least 12½-gauge woven wire. In most residential areas, however, such a fence is not permissible by law. In areas where this fence is legal, construction costs prove to be quite high.

Some building codes permit the use of an outrigger structure on a low fence. This design is based on the observation that deer are better high jumpers than broad jumpers. To deer-proof a 4½-foot-high fence, build an 8-foot lean-to outrigger from the top of the fence to the ground. For the outrigger, use 9-foot steel fence posts spaced 12 feet apart, and string 10-gauge wire between the posts at 6 and 12-inch intervals as shown on the next page.

The outrigger is always built outward from the fence, so it's a good idea to make sure you own the necessary 8 feet of property on the other side of the existing fence before constructing a permanent structure.

Other observations have been made about deer. They seem to shy away of paving that is close to a fence, and baffle fences seem to be effective, because the deer are apparently frightened by a maze.

If you are considering building a deer fence, it would be a good idea to drop a note to your State Fish and Game Department. Most states with heavy deer populations publish helpful information on deer fencing.

CHOICES OF DEER FENCING

Keeping deer out of an orchard or garden often calls for special fencing measures. Because deer crawl between the strands, regular stock fences of barbed wire are not effective and installation of electric fences is generally costly.

Wire mesh fences 8 feet high (higher in areas of heavy snowfall) are usually the most effective, but these can also be quite expensive. There are less expensive alternatives. Where lower fences already exist, extensions of supports and wire mesh may be added either vertically or "overhanging" (at an outward angle), or outrigger structures may be built outward from the top of the fence to the ground.

Some people prefer to simply encircle prized plants and tender tree trunks with protective wire cylinders, leaving the lower leaves and fruit to be pruned off by the deer.

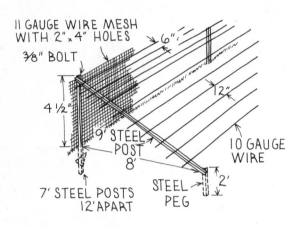

OUTRIGGERS will foil deer where you want to keep fence low for view. Fence is only 4½ feet high, has 9-foot steel outriggers extending 8 feet out.

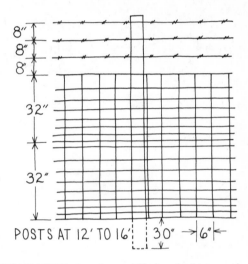

ECONOMICAL deer fence (7½ feet high) is made of two 32-inch rolls of poultry fencing, topped with three barbed strands. Posts are 12 to 16 feet apart.

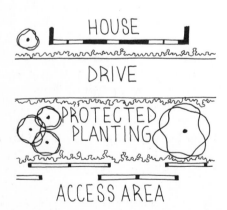

BAFFLES or mazes are often very effective for deer control because deer shy away from them. They also tend to stay away from paved areas.

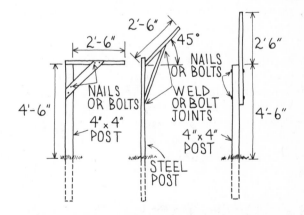

CONVERTING an existing fence into a deer fence can be done as shown in these drawings. In regions with heavy snows, higher fences may be required.

SLAT SCREEN, plants, form background for natural wood sculpture.

Fence Plantings, Lighting, Decoration

A newly constructed fence is likely to have a stark appearance even though it was planned to fit into your garden. One way to break up a long and monotonous expanse of lumber surrounding you is through the use of imaginative planting and landscaping. If the fence serves mainly as the wall of an outdoor room, any number of decorative possibilities (such as sand castings, paintings, mosaics, or sculptures) may be added for color, interest, or a note of whimsy. Assuming the planting and/or decoration is attractive, it is often then a good idea to install dramatic lighting—so that the fence may enhance the garden after dark.

Plants Add Life to a Fence

Neither plants nor fences should normally be left standing alone in a garden. Plants can help a fence become an integrated part of the landscape by softening the stern lines of the structure. Also, a planted fence is cooler, both in appearance and

function, than one of bare boards. Covered with thick, leafy vines or espaliered plants, it will often shade a sunny section of the garden area from the direct rays of the hot summer sun. Plants can also add new patterns, textures, and color accents to existing fences.

A fence, in turn, focuses attention on the plants in front of it. A fence also acts as a windbreak, creating a haven of quiet air on the lee side. Heat is reflected and stored on the sunny side of a fence, and even an open rail fence deflects the flow of freezing air that causes plant damage. On the north or east side of a house, shade-loving plants flourish behind the shelter of a fence.

How well shrubs and vines will do against a fence depends quite a bit upon the exposure of the structure. Plants that normally thrive in full sun may literally bake when grown against west and south-facing surfaces. This is especially true when the surface is white or light in color.

One way to decrease the heat reflection of such a fence is to remove one or two boards for air circulation. Another way to provide air circulation is to train plants against a trellis that is positioned a few inches from the surface of the fence.

Here are some general points to guide you in the selection of the right plants for your particular fence, climate, and landscape.

For delicately constructed fences of wire mesh, plastic screen, thin lath, or bamboo stakes, use vines and shrubs that create a light and graceful pattern. If your fence has a distinctive pattern or finish, a heavy mass of green leaves will blot it out. Bear in mind that some plants are very sturdy, and the more aggressive varieties can wrench apart a lightly constructed fence.

For heavily constructed fences of solid panels, board, or rough grapestakes, use vines and shrubs that have large thick leaves or bushy masses of finer foliage. Dark, solid fences that seem too massive can be made more attractive by using low to medium plants in the foreground with light, gray-foliaged shrubs. A single solid panel makes a good backdrop for displaying plants, particularly those that you want to highlight, or those that might get lost if planted among other foliage. Even though you might prefer evergreen plants, don't overlook the design value of bare winter branches followed by the refreshing effect of spring foliage.

In narrow planting spaces along a fence, espaliered shrubs are a logical choice. Fruit trees are especially popular in this type of situation—they are easy to control and you can grow them to yield a few special prizes. When your fence is exposed to the full rays of the sun, leave space between the fence and plants or they may burn in the reflected heat. In areas where citrus is marginally successful, fruit trees will flourish against a fence section of heat-retaining glass or plastic.

For training plants against a fence, use soft, non-cutting materials to tie them in place—raffia, cloth, rubber strips, or coated wire are good. Supporting wire can be bare, but under bright sunlight it may heat up enough to burn tender shoots. Insulated wire and plastic clothesline won't heat and are strong enough to keep most climbing plants standing straight up.

Plants that twine or cling are easier to manage than stiff, floppy branches that have to be tied or stapled again and again. Fence plantings take more grooming than other plants to keep them from running wild. Also, if you plan to repaint your fence, you'll have to take the vines down from time to time.

OPEN FRAMEWORK of pipe and wood is transformed into a carport screen by climbing bougainvillea.

NARROW PLANTING BED beside fence offered enough space for podocarpus hedge; thrives on deep watering.

CLIMBING IVY gives three dimensional effect to flat surface of screen made of medium-sized wood slats.

LIVING ART IN THE GARDEN

Espaliering plants, vines, or shrubs for a formal appearance requires a good deal of exacting patience in pruning and training in order to achieve a rigid symmetry. Plants which have been informally espaliered are more carefree and cover a fence or screen casually. Which style you ultimately choose—formal or informal—will depend upon the style of your garden and the feeling you wish to create.

The informal espaliers can provide a thick, bushy surface covering or an irregular tracery. They still need control, however. The bushier the plant, the more it will need frequent snipping, pinching, or pruning of side shoots and leaf buds to keep it close to the surface it is to cover.

In some areas, plants too tender for exposed situations can thrive when espaliered against sheltered fences, patio walls, or on house walls under a roof overhang.

PYRACANTHA, espaliered here on grapestake fence, grows easily, has flowers in summer, winter berries.

INFORMAL ESPALIER of Camellia sasanqua grows on a screen of 1 by 2's, adds to privacy for entry.

LIVING SCULPTURE of gray-leafed santolina makes an attractive base for uniquely-styled post and rail.

KIWI—A DELICIOUS NEWCOMER

Newly available to home gardeners is the Kiwi vine *(Actinidia chinensis)*. Particularly adaptable to planting alongside fences or screens, the Kiwi (also known as the Chinese gooseberry or Yang-tao vine) is an attractive vine with big, roundish, dark green leaves. Its structure is more open than grape vines, but provides a strong, bold pattern against a fence. Leaves stay on the vines until fall.

In May the Kiwi bears clusters of white flowers (which gradually turn to buff). The fruits begin to develop soon after but do not ripen until late fall.

The fuzzy, brown-skinned fruit is rather unattractive, but the delicious flavor of the pale green flesh has been described as a blend of melon, strawberry, and banana.

Only the female Kiwi plant bears fruit, and only when there is a male plant nearby. The Kiwi cannot endure continued hard freezes, and late frosts can damage blossoms and young fruit.

FRUIT OF KIWI is brown and furry. Flesh is pale green, shading to cream; it has a delicious taste.

FLOWERS of plant open white, fade to buff. Female plant flower is shown at right, male flower at left.

VINES TWINE along rail of this post and board fence, softening its lines and changing its personality.

VARIETY OF PLANTINGS enhance solid face of tall slat fence. Espaliered pear tree is near the gate.

VINES CLIMB informally up slat fence that sits on top of concrete wall framed with wood strips.

SOLID BOARD FENCE recedes into the background, doesn't compete for attention with blooming azaleas.

IVY CLIMBS easily over fence, grows out of planter box which is attached to bottom of large gates.

CHAMFERED AND NOTCHED 4 by 4 posts and 2 by 2's projecting above fence stand out sharply against wall.

APPLE TREE is handsomely espaliered on shiplap fence which matches house. Open post and rail tops fence.

AIRY QUALITY in fence is achieved by not extending posts to top, hiding them behind notched 1 by 6's.

CAST CONCRETE BLOCKS, embellished with stones, bits of mosaic, chandelier crystals, decorate fence.

ESPALIERED FIGS have lush foliage in summer, reveal branch patterns in winter. 1 by 4's let air circulate.

WHIMSICAL PANEL of concrete bird, river stone eggs is held against fence by two 1¼ inch angle iron posts.

Special Effects—Fence Decoration

There are times when the stark appearance of large, bare expanses of fences cannot be relieved solely by plants. This is especially true in a new garden where plants need time for growth in order to enhance the appearance of the fence.

Fence and screen decoration is an alternative for those who wish an immediate relief from their bareness or who like the combination of plants and decorative elements. Decoration not only adds color and interest, but makes a fence seem more like the wall of a room.

In working with outdoor rooms, different factors must be considered than those prevalent with indoor rooms. With the sky for the ceiling and a long, distant fence as a wall, an object such as a picture intended for use indoors would be lost outdoors. Normally, a person stands farther from a fence than from an indoor wall, so the outdoor scale should be larger.

Weathering should also be kept in mind when considering outdoor decorations for fences and screens. Materials used should be able to take the extremes of sun, wind, rain, and temperature. On the other hand, weathering of some materials can be attractive if it doesn't affect the structural strength. Wood, copper, brass, bronze, and brick often become more attractive as they weather.

Use of Night Lighting

The installation of night lighting can add another dimension to the overall effect of fence plantings and decoration. Fences, gates, and screens are ideal structures for mounting electrical fixtures or hiding reflectors, lamps, and light bulbs. Many gardens look much more dramatic at night with some judicious placing of lights to highlight the attractive features and subdue less attractive areas.

A fence is a natural background for silhouetted plants, and the shadow patterns of branches and leaves against panels add interest to gardens. A soft glow of light diffused through a plastic panel is another exciting way to achieve night effects. For temporary decorative needs, such as a party, a fence is a part of your garden that can easily be dressed up without damage.

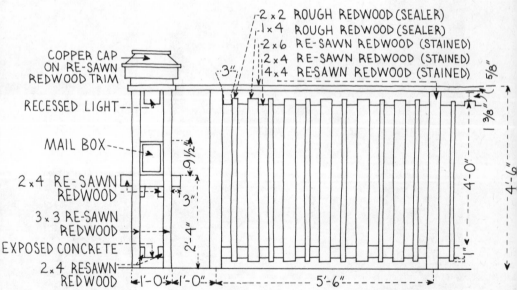

NIGHT LIGHTING is provided by incorporating a fixture into this gatepost. Light bulb was easily concealed in the decorative cap, illuminates the address, makes the entryway seem much friendlier.

SOFTLY LIGHTED small courtyard was created by placing a translucent screen between windows and carport.

DRAMATIC EFFECT is created by placing lights behind translucent plastic fence panel, silhouetting plants.

GLASS FLOATS give curved screen a highly decorative touch. They are glued to short lengths of 2 by 4's.

FIRED CLAY TILES are wired together and attached to iron bars inside wood frame; breeze makes them ring.

DECORATIVE ELEMENTS in this fence include colored glass inserts in plastic, jauntily balanced caps.

WOOD GATE softens solid effect of adjacent brick wall.

Gates...
Ornate and Simple

Gates often have definite personalities which can affect the whole feeling and mood of a house and garden. They must therefore be planned and designed with care.

A gate usually tells something about the people who live in the house beyond it. It is the first thing visitors encounter, and the visual impression can be inviting or forbidding, formal or informal, romantic or functional.

The type of fence you are building will, of course, influence your choice of gates. But this does not mean that the gate has to be of the same material or design. By altering the design slightly, you can make the gate stand out without creating too sharp a contrast. For example, in a fence with vertically placed pickets or boards, the gate can be given a horizontal or criss-cross construction, or the pickets or boards can be spaced differently. On the other hand, there are situations where it is desirable to play down the gate and design it so that its position in the fence is hardly noticeable except for its latch or a path leading to it. This is usually done by incorporating the same materials and design of the fence into the gate.

The ease of entering through a gate depends upon its design, weight, and size. The way it is mounted may also affect passage through it. A single gate with hinges on one side, and a latch on the other is the most familiar mounting method, but it may be hung as a single or double swinging gate, or as a double gate with conventional hinges and latches.

Gate Size

The size of a gate should be determined by the height of the fence it serves and the degree of security desired. It should be in scale with its surroundings. A low, inadequate front gate is an annoyance, and a challenge to budding young hurdlers. Oversize gates, on the other hand, may seem ostentatious or institutional in character.

Some gates, of course, defy originality in design. The ones that come complete from the factory are only as adaptable as the range of plans in the catalog. Gates that serve strictly utilitarian purposes, such as those that close the pasture, orchard, or barnyard, look best if they do their job honestly.

But, whether gates are ornate or simple, high or low, owner-built or prefabricated, they must meet one common requirement—they have to work.

Plan for Wear and Tear

Gates get more wear and abuse than any other part of the fence, and if they are expected to last, they must be built solidly and attached with top quality, heavy-duty hardware. When you put in a header board along a path, or nail lath on a trellis, a small error can be made here and there and no one will know the difference. But a few miscalculations or a little bad workmanship on a gate and you end up with one that doesn't close; or worse, one that won't open in wet weather.

To avoid these pitfalls, plan your gate carefully. A good first step, particularly if the project is complex is to make a sketch of your proposed gate and show it to a local lumber dealer. He can usually tell whether your plan is feasible, how much it will cost, and whether there's some way to make the job easier by modifying the design slightly. Before you make a sketch, however, you'll have to know something about gate construction. There are three considerations; the latch, the hinges, and the gate itself.

Choice of latches. Although it may seem like putting the cart before the horse, the first thing to consider is the latch. In many cases, the gate must be built around the latch, unless it's a simple hasp or hook. For example, a sliding bolt action latch may be too difficult to install on a gate with grapestake siding. Check hardware and lumber supply stores for latch ideas. Sketches of some of the most commonly used latches are shown on page 95. You can have more ornate latches made to order. Wooden latches, designed as part of the

WARM AND FRIENDLY look of this gate is achieved with combination of lattice and solid board, warm bricks.

COOL, YET BECKONING black iron gate has straight lines to contrast dramatically with white stuccoed house.

RUGGED, handsome gate can be constructed by using standard chain link framework and facing it with boards, in this case alternate redwood widths. Wide and narrow gates were installed side by side.

ROUGH, WEATHERED LUMBER forms deer fence and gate. Shadows formed by sunlight offer continual delight.

ORNAMENTAL GATE was once the door of old-fashioned cage elevator.

MASSIVE double wooden gate spans five-foot opening, swings from heavy wood strips bolted to brick wall.

OLD JAPANESE GATE leads to enclosed Japanese garden. Board fence was designed around gate.

OPEN SCREEN gate has doorbell on post at right. When bell rings, owner releases gate catch automatically.

ORNATELY CARVED, this gate harmonizes with handsomely detailed woodwork over front door of the house.

CEDAR GRILLE made of 1 by 2's forms gate of grapestake fence. Effect is informal, invites you in.

ENTRY GATE leads to covered entry, can be locked to keep children in, uninvited out, yet looks friendly.

gate, are fun to devise, do not rust, and are easily replaced if they wear out or break.

Remember that the latch must take rough treatment. A flimsy one, put on with small nails or screws, won't last long. If you want to keep children from opening the gate, get a latch that you can set up high or on top of the fence.

Choice of hinges. The principal cause of gate failure is inadequate hinges. It is better to choose an overly strong hinge than one not strong enough. Hinges, like latches, have to be considered in terms of the gate siding. It would be impossible, for ex-

ample, to mount heavy strap hinges on a gate paneled in translucent plastic. Sometimes you'll want to buy hinges that match the latch, which may call for a revision in the gate design. If a fence is used to confine small children, self-closing hinges are a worthwhile investment. Springs in the hinge mechanism automatically close the gate, which otherwise might be left ajar by visitors or deliverymen.

Some of the more familiar hinges are illustrated below. All of them do a good job, providing they are sized for the weight of the gate, and if you use screws that are long enough. Many of the packaged

HOW TO BUILD A GATE

Ornate or simple, all gates must meet one common requirement—they must work simply and easily. Building a good, workable gate requires extra care and attention to detail. Here is a gate building project for you to follow—from the first step straight through to the self-satisfying stage of opening and closing the gate for the first time. The steps are as follows:

1. **Determine the gate size.** First measure the space between the gate posts at both the top and the bottom (if it varies considerably you'll have to plumb the posts before you can hang a gate). Plan your frame width one inch less than this opening—for a three-foot opening the width of your frame should be 35" to give swing and hinge space (for gates built of heavy material, allow slightly more space to assure free swinging).

2. **Build the frame.** The simplest way to do this is on a work table or any flat surface. The joints may be either simply lapped or mortised (see page 23). When nailing the frame pieces together, be sure to keep the frame at right angles with a square.

3. **Attach a diagonal brace.** Place the frame on a 2 by 4 (to be used as the brace) and pencil

in the sawing marks. For a tight fit, saw the 2 by 4 so that you leave the pencil marks on the brace. Attach the brace at both ends by nailing through both the horizontal and vertical rails.

4. **Attach the siding.** Starting at the hinge side of the frame, nail boards or pickets as determined by spacing design and spacing. The distances between pickets or the widths of solid boards may have to be varied from the rest of the fence to get even spacing. (Siding can also be attached after the gate is hung if the completed gate will be too heavy to be manageable otherwise.)

5. **Attach the hinges.** Drill nail and screw holes with a drill that's slightly smaller in diameter than the fastenings. (Use galvanized or other non-corroding hardware in building your gate.)

6. **Fit the gate.** Hold the gate in place. If it is too close to the posts to swing freely, trim the edge of the gate which swings open until it fits.

7. **Attach the hinges.** Prop the gate in place with wood blocks to hold it in proper position and attach the hinges' loose ends to the post.

8. **Attach the latch.** Use long screws or bolts, because the latch often takes quite a beating.

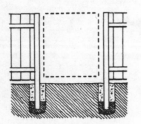
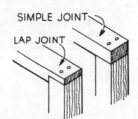
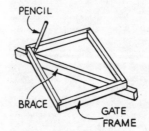
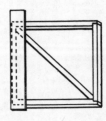

ACCURATE PLANS are necessary in order to build a strong and working gate. For a tight-fitting diagonal brace, mark lines as shown and saw on the outer edge of the marks.

TRIM, LOUVERED gate is as functional as the wall; it relieves the massive, unfriendly look of the brick.

SPANISH GATE complements the garden beyond. Ivy and azaleas (left), boxwood, and fuchsias frame gate.

DOWELS form an open, friendly entry gate which permits view of court but provides sense of security.

WIDE GATE to Japanese-styled garden is subtle in design, blends in with tall trees, vertical structures.

hinges include screws that are too short for a heavy gate. Use screws that go as far into the wood as possible, without coming out the other side. Always use three hinges on gates that are over five feet tall. Buy only hinges with a weather-resistant coating—cadmium, zinc, or galvanized—unless you plan on painting them; otherwise they'll rust and streak your gate.

Choice of materials. In selecting the material for your gate, you have the same choices as in fence siding. Most gates have 2 by 4-inch frames, covered with facing material. Lighter frames can be used if the siding is exterior plywood or some other light material. These won't sag, but they usually need support on the flat sides to keep them from bowing and to give you a place to fasten hinges and latches. Don't buy warped lumber. It doesn't take much of a curve to throw the whole gate out of line. Sometimes you may have to go through half a dozen pieces before finding a straight one. If you have to buy green lumber, let it dry out for at least a week before you use it. Lay the boards on blocks to let the air circulate around the wood.

MORE THAN ONE WAY TO CROSS A FENCE

There are certain situations where a gate is not desired for aesthetic purposes or cannot be used because of vine or plant growth on it or nearby.

Illustrated are two different types of stiles which might be considered in lieu of gates. One particular advantage of a stile is that it can provide needed access temporarily whereas a gate is a very permanent fixture.

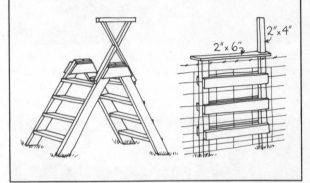

GALVANIZED STEEL PICKETS painted black, are set three inches apart in frame of 3 by 6-inch redwood.

WROUGHT IRON GATE picks up round design in fence, contrasts pleasantly with white of the concrete.

HOW TO FIX A SAGGING GATE

Garden and entry gates normally take a sound beating. They're exposed to wind and weather, young gate swingers, and hurried deliverymen who often push against the framework before the latch is free. Gates hung from fences that are not very rigid, and which tend to expand and contract with the weather, often bind, refuse to latch, and drag on the ground. If you have one or more of these gate problems, the following checklist should help you to pinpoint and correct the situation:

1. Check the hinges. Loose hinges should be replaced with larger hinges or the screws replaced

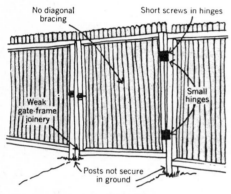

Common gate problems

with longer ones or even bolts (many of the screws that come with hinge sets are too short). Gates more than 5 feet high or wider than 3 feet should have three hinges. Two weak hinges can be strengthened with a third one of similar size, placed between the other two and a bit above the mid point.

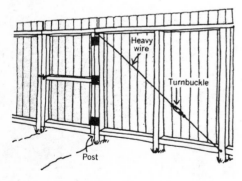

Turnbuckle and heavy wire

2. Check the posts. A leaning hinge-side post is another major cause of trouble. It not only carries the weight of the gate, but also the weight of anyone swinging on it. If the post is leaning, you may be able to remedy the problem simply by straightening it up and tamping the soil around it. But this may turn out to be only a temporary remedy. If it hasn't been set in concrete, it probably should be. If the post has simply leaned straight over from the weight of the gate, you can straighten and hold it with a turnbuckle and heavy wire or threaded steel rod running to the bottom of another post down the fence line as shown. These straightening methods can also be used on the latch-side post.

3. Check the gate itself. Most gates aren't overly strong to begin with and will sag out of shape when subjected to the weather. A wire and turnbuckle which runs opposite to the diagonal wood brace (the wire should run from the hinge

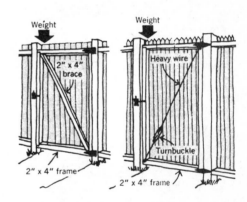

Two ways to brace a gate

side on top to the latch side at the bottom) will pull the gate back into place. The wire and turnbuckle are superior to the 2 by 4 bracing because they're lighter and also adjustable. (Turnbuckle kits, containing turnbuckle, heavy wire or threaded rods, and metal angle plates, are available at many hardware stores.) If the gate binds in wet weather, but works nicely during warm seasons, plane off a little of the latch post or gate frame to give at least a 1/4-inch clearance for expansion. Conversely, if the gate has shrunk so that the latch will not catch you will have to either relocate it or replace it with a latch having a longer reach. If the gate has sunk straight down, simply reset the hinges or the latch.

JAPANESE GATE hints at what is beyond. Built of 1 by 12's with bamboo poles, the gate's outside latch (right) is part of handle. Inside, the handle/latch (center) is bolted to other end of 1/4-inch pipe.

CHINESE MOON GATE is round bronze grille. Design is inviting, is often used to frame a garden view.

SCROLLED WROUGHT IRON GATE opens into entry court which was formed when brick wall joined house.

SEE-THROUGH GATE permits view of steps on other side. Scroll-sawn design complements brick wall.

HARDWARE FOR GARDEN GATES

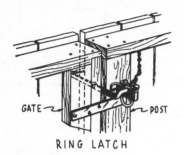

GATE —| |— POST

RING LATCH

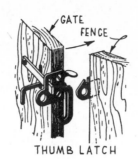

GATE
FENCE

THUMB LATCH

GATE

PULL STRING TO OPEN

SELF LATCHING

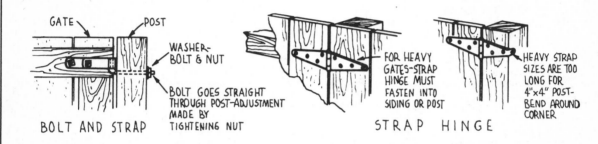

GATE — POST

WASHER-BOLT & NUT

BOLT GOES STRAIGHT THROUGH POST—ADJUSTMENT MADE BY TIGHTENING NUT

BOLT AND STRAP

FOR HEAVY GATES—STRAP HINGE MUST FASTEN INTO SIDING OR POST

HEAVY STRAP SIZES ARE TOO LONG FOR 4"x4" POST- BEND AROUND CORNER

STRAP HINGE

HASP LATCH

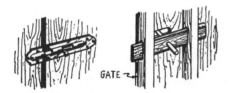

GATE

BOLT ACTION LATCHES

GATE

TOP LATCH

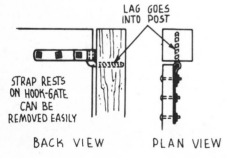

LAG GOES INTO POST

STRAP RESTS ON HOOK-GATE CAN BE REMOVED EASILY

BACK VIEW   **PLAN VIEW**

LAG AND STRAP

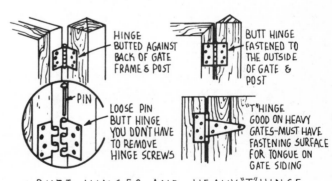

HINGE BUTTED AGAINST BACK OF GATE FRAME & POST

BUTT HINGE FASTENED TO THE OUTSIDE OF GATE & POST

PIN

LOOSE PIN BUTT HINGE YOU DON'T HAVE TO REMOVE HINGE SCREWS

"T" HINGE GOOD ON HEAVY GATES-MUST HAVE FASTENING SURFACE FOR TONGUE ON GATE SIDING

BUTT HINGES AND HEAVY "T" HINGE

Photo Credits

Jerry A. Anson: pages 38 (left), 49 (bottom left). **William Aplin:** pages 33 (bottom left), 36 (bottom left), 41 (top right), 43 (left), 48 (bottom left), 75 (left), 79 (right), 80 (center right), 82 (top left). **Morley Baer:** pages 9 (bottom), 40 (center right), 87 (right). **Baldinger Photo:** page 78. **Nancy Bannick:** page 58 (center right). **Douglas Baylis:** page 49 (top right). **Jeremiah O. Bragstad:** pages 48 (top left), 92 (left). **Ernest Braun:** pages 51 (top right, center left), 70 (top), 91 (top left). **Tom Burns Jr.:** page 9 (top). **Cal Pictures:** page 64 (bottom). **Clyde Childress:** pages 63 (left), 81 (bottom right), 86. **Childress-Halberstadt:** page 51 (bottom left). **Glenn Christiansen:** pages 57, 85 (bottom left), 89 (bottom left), 94 (top). **Robert C. Cleveland:** page 41 (bottom left). **Nancy Davidson:** page 88 (bottom right). **Dick Dawson:** page 79 (left). **Brent Dickens:** page 84. **Douglas Ebersole:** pages 55 (left), 56 (top left). **Carol Eyerman:** page 37 (bottom right). **Philip Fein:** pages 48 (top right), 49 (center left). **Richard Fish:** pages 12 (top), 59 (bottom left, top left), 64 (top), 69 (left, right), 70 (center left, center right), 72 (bottom left, bottom right), 73 (center right), 74, 82 (bottom left), 83 (bottom left), 94 (bottom left). **Bert Goldrath:** page 59 (bottom right). **Howard Hoffman:** pages 37 (bottom left), 40 (top right). **Art Hupy:** pages 81 (top), 94 (bottom right). **Philip Hyde:** page 88 (center right). **Don Jaenicke:** pages 41 (center left), 51 (center right, bottom right). **Lee Klein:** pages 4, 13 (bottom), 14, 30, 32 (top left, top right, center left), 34 (top), 36 (top left, top right, center right, bottom right), 37 (top left, top right), 40 (top left, bottom left), 41 (top left), 42 (top, bottom), 44 (top), 45 (center, bottom), 46 (left, right), 48 (bottom right, 49 (top left), 50 (top, center left, bottom left, bottom right), 54, 56 (top right, center left, center right, bottom), 58 (top), 60, 62, 63 (right), 68, 70 (bottom right), 71 (top left, bottom right), 75 (right), 85 (top left, bottom right), 88 (top, bottom left), 89 (top left). **Roy Krell:** pages 45 (top), 58 (center left), 61 (bottom right), 72 (top right), 73 (bottom), 82 (bottom right), 83 (top right), 85 (center left). **Dearborn Massar:** page 61 (bottom left, center left). **Jack McDowell:** page 18. **Michael and Steve McKeag:** page 39. **Don Normark:** pages 12 (bottom), 50 (center right), 51 (top left), 58 (bottom), 59 (center right), 73 (center left), 80 (top, bottom left), 82 (top right), 89 (top right, center left). **Phil Palmer:** page 70 (bottom left). **Ron Partridge:** page 41 (bottom right). **Selwyn Pullan:** page 55 (right). **John Robinson:** pages 38 (right), 44 (center, bottom), 49, (center right). **Martha Rosman:** pages 40 (bottom right), 59 (top right), 83 (bottom right), 89 (bottom right), 91 (bottom left). **Julius Shulman:** pages 9 (center), 65. **Blair Stapp:** page 83 (center right). **Hugh N. Stratford:** pages 49 (bottom right), 91 (top left). **George R. Szanik:** page 94 (center right). **Max Tach:** page 32 (bottom right). **Mike Tilden:** page 81 (bottom left). **Darrow Watt:** pages 43 (right), 72 (top left), 81 (center left), 91 (top right). **Elton Welke:** page 61 (center right). **R. Wenkam:** page 40 (center left). **Mason Weymouth:** pages 37 (center left), 83 (top left), 87 (left).